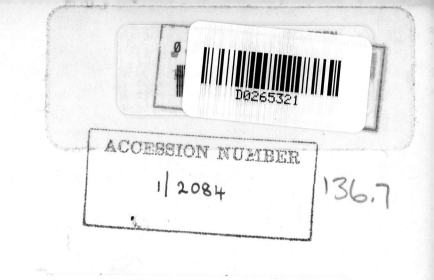

BASIC BOOKS IN EDUCATION

Editor: *Kathleen O'Connor, B.Sc., Senior Lecturer in Education, Rolle College, Exmouth*
Advisory Editor: *D. J. O'Connor, M.A., Ph.D., Professor of Philosophy, University of Exeter*

An Introduction to - Human Development

Second edition

Dr. Lovell considers seven major areas of human development which are of particular relevance to teachers, college of education students and social workers. Current views are presented clearly and succinctly and the book provides a wide but accurate coverage of the field. There are two hundred references to enable readers to follow up particular issues.

Advantage has been taken in the second edition of clarifying a few points, of expanding others with the aid of fresh material, and of including a number of new and important references which were not available at the time the first edition went to press.

Key words are in SMALL CAPITALS, there is a 'further reading' list at the end of each chapter, a full bibliography, glossary and an index.

An Introduction to Human Development

K. LOVELL, B.Sc., M.A., Ph.D.

READER IN EDUCATION, UNIVERSITY OF LEEDS

MACMILLAN

© K. Lovell 1968, 1969

first edition 1968
second edition 1969

Published by
MACMILLAN AND CO LTD
Little Essex Street London W C 2
and also at Bombay Calcutta and Madras
Macmillan South Africa (Publishers) Pty Ltd Johannesburg
The Macmillan Company of Australia Pty Ltd Melbourne
The Macmillan Company of Canada Ltd Toronto
Gill and Macmillan Ltd Dublin

Printed in Great Britain by
ROBERT MACLEHOSE AND CO LTD
The University Press, Glasgow

Contents

Preface

It is hoped that this book will serve as a text in Colleges of Education and University Departments of Education. It is also hoped that it will prove valuable, as an introductory text, for students who are preparing for the B.Ed. Degree, or for an Advanced Diploma or Higher Degree in Education. But it should also be of help to medical students, nurses, social workers, parents, and all who are interested in children's development.

Readers are asked to keep in mind two points when using this book. First, it has been necessary to make drastic selections from the voluminous literature in order to keep the book within the size stipulated by the publisher. But two hundred references are included in the Further Reading sections and Bibliography so that any topic may be studied further. Second, there is as yet no conceptual framework inside which the various aspects of developmental psychology can be discussed. This being so, the subject matter of the chapters cannot, as present, always be made to link easily.

K. LOVELL

1 Biological Development

We begin our discussion of human development by very briefly considering the mechanism of human heredity. The NUCLEI of human CELLS usually contain twenty-three pairs of threadlike structures called CHROMOSOMES on which are located the GENES, although in the case of sex cells (ova and sperm) there is only half this number because only one of each pair is present. It is now thought that the genes are large and complex molecules of deoxyribonucleic acid (DNA), the latter being associated with the way in which information is coded for genetic purposes, that is, for the purposes of influencing, say, physical features and growth, temperament and so forth (4).

When the egg cell from the mother's ovary and the sperm from the father's testes fuse to form a fertilised ovum or ZYGOTE, one member of each chromosome pair is contributed by each of the parents. The zygote, now containing the full twenty-three pairs of chromosomes, divides into two cells, then into four, then into eight and so on up to billions of cells that make up the body. The resulting cells soon begin to assume special functions as parts of the circulatory, muscular, nervous and skeletal systems. So the genetic content which is bequeathed at the moment of fertilisation from each parent pervades the whole being of the new individual, the genes exerting their influence on the growing organism through the control of various biochemical reactions which are involved in the growth and functioning of the individual. The organism's genetic constitution or its GENOTYPE interacts continuously with the environment to bring about the resulting PHENOTYPE, or observable characteristics, such as intelligence. It is obvious that it is not the phenotype that is inherited but only the genetic constitution.

Human traits such as intelligence or emotional stability which are of the greatest interest to us in education, can be considered as due, in part, to many pairs of genes (polygenes) producing effects which are cumulative. Such traits are in the child to a greater or lesser degree rather than being present or absent, so that we see graded variations of the trait in the children we teach. A feature of the polygenes is that their measurable or phenotypic expression is greatly affected by environmental conditions from birth onwards. However, we have, as yet, little exact knowledge concerning the ways in which the genotype may be favourably influenced so as to result in an improved phenotype, although there is a body of knowledge accumulating in respect of the kind of environment that adversely affects the genotype.

Determination of sex

The sex of a child is determined the moment a sperm fuses with the ovum. Fifty per cent of all sperms each contain what is termed an X chromosome, and the other half each contains a Y chromosome, while all egg cells or ova contain one X chromosome each. When a sperm carrying an X chromosome unites with an egg cell, the zygote contains two X chromosomes and the child is a female. But when a sperm carrying a Y chromosome unites with an egg cell, the fertilised ovum contains an X and a Y chromosome and the offspring is male. Later we shall see that there are a few children who do not conform to this pattern of sex chromosomes.

Identical and fraternal twins

Occasionally two ova are fertilised each by a different sperm at almost the same time. The two embryos develop into what are called dizygotic or fraternal twins and they may be of unlike sex. From the point of view of heredity they have no more in common than brothers and sisters, although they may experience a greater similarity in environmental influences if reared together than would be the case with ordinary siblings. More rarely, however, the first two cells formed from the zygote part and each gives rise to independent embryos. The latter develop into monozygotic or identical twins, each twin receiving an assortment of genes exactly like that of the other. When identical twins are reared apart a good opportunity is provided to study the relative effect of genetic and environmental influences. However, while this approach does enable one to study the effects of these two influences, it is now realised that there are certain difficulties in using the method that were not recognised a few years ago. For example, it is now known that the genes alone are not responsible for heredity, the CYTOPLASM or the relatively clear substance separated from the cell nucleus by a membrane, also plays a part. Again, the prenatal environment of monozygotic twins may differ from that of dizygotic twins. For example, Sydow and Rinne (123) have shown that a pair of monozygotic twins differed markedly in haemoglobin values and weight during at least the first ten months of life.

The inheritance of acquired characteristics

A question of great general interest is whether characteristics that have been acquired by a person during life can be passed on to his children through the mechanism of heredity. In the view of western scientists it is unlikely that the transmission of acquired characteristics is possible in this way. When some special skill or characteristic is noted in both parent and child, it is likely that the potentiality for the skill or characteristic was transmitted to the child and that a favourable environment and opportunities, such as watching his parent, or playing alongside him, produced the phenotype.

PHYSICAL DEVELOPMENT

Neonatal period

Some four weeks after conception foetal heartbeat commences, at four to five months definite foetal movements are reported by the mother, and between the fifth and sixth month it is possible to evoke respiratory movements in the foetus. Normal birth occurs about 280 days from the end of the last menstrual period before conception and the four weeks following a full-term delivery is known as the neonatal period. This is a period during which the child has to make certain physiological adjustments to his new environment; for example, his breathing and body temperature settle at steady values.

As early as the first week of life children differ among themselves in a number of ways. Some lie still and quiet, others show considerable arm and leg movement. The degree to which the baby shows such motor activity may affect the way his parents react to him and hence his subsequent development may be influenced. In this neonatal period infants show great differences in respect of the degree of stimulation required in the auditory, olfactory, tactile and visual modalities to elicit a response. Newborn children also show differences in the way they react to stress, e.g. hunger; these reactions are reflected in changes in the cardiovascular system, the gastrointestinal tract, the respiratory system and the skin. Such differences are not necessarily due to heredity, they may be due at least in part, to the intrauterine environment and development. In addition we do not know whether the physiological reactivity of the newborn correlates highly with that of the older child. As already mentioned, if such reactivity in the newborn remains constant for, say, one year, the child's whole future development may be affected. For it might influence the infant's interaction with the environment, and the reactions of adults to him.

Physical growth

At birth the average full-term boy, who is slightly larger in all body dimensions than the average full-term girl, weighs $7\frac{1}{2}$ lb and is about 20 inches in length. Around one-quarter of the total length is head, while the remainder is divided equally between limbs and trunk. By 5 years of age the average child is some 43 to 44 inches tall, but only one-eighth of this is head, while the legs take up more than half of the remainder. Thus the 5-year-old has quite a different shape from a newborn baby. Between about 3 and 10 years of age overall growth takes place at a fairly constant rate. Indeed Tanner (124) suggests that the simple mathematical curve

$$\text{Height} = a + bt + ct^2$$

fits the data for height in centimetres and *t* in years over the age range indicated above.[1]

However, by 9 years of age or soon after, important physical changes may take place in the girl, although it must be stressed that for some quite normal girls such changes may not take place until 13 or even later. The first signs of approaching puberty, that is, the age at which the individual is capable of reproduction, are the slight enlargement of breasts and the appearance of hair underneath the arms and on the pubes. At about the same time the hips grow faster than the shoulders, the amount of fat on the limbs and trunk increases, and there is a general acceleration of growth which is known as the adolescent spurt. From between one and two years after the growth spurt beginning, the rate of growth commences to slow down and by about this time the growth of the breasts and genital organs is complete. Menarche does not occur until most of the growth spurt is over. Even so, the first menstrual cycles do not herald complete sexual maturity and ability to reproduce since ova are not normally liberated by the ovaries.

As in so many human characteristics there is much individual variation. Within a classroom containing girls of the same chronological age there will be some who have reached adolescence and begun to menstruate while others show signs neither of sexual maturity nor of the spurt in growth. The early maturing girls will, on the average, be bigger and stronger than the later developing ones. Moreover the average girl at 11 will be bigger and stronger than the average boy of the same chronological age since the adolescent growth spurt for the male comes later. It is now generally known that the age of menarche has been decreasing for a century or more in Western Europe and in the USA. In Britain the average age for the onset of menstruation is now a little over 13 years, with the normal range, for 95 per cent of all girls, running from 10 to 15 years. Thus a number of girls may have begun to menstruate before they leave the primary school at 11 + years of age. The reasons for this decrease in the age of menarche are unclear and a number of possible causes have been suggested. There is likewise no agreed opinion as to whether or not the downward trend is currently continuing.

The adolescent growth spurt in boys commences around 12 to 13 years of age although once again there are great individual differences. The boys' growth spurt is greater and possibly more sustained, so that they are eventually some 10 per cent larger than girls in most dimensions. The breadth of the chest and shoulders show large increases in the male. Again, compared with the girl, the amount of bone and muscle in a boy's body increases considerably, but fat decreases. The first sign of puberty in the boy is usually an acceleration of the growth of the testes and scrotum. The larynx grows larger a little after the spurt in height, and there is a deepening of the voice at about the time the growth of the genitalia is nearing completion. As the muscles of the back, chest and shoulder grow in boys, the strength of their arm pull and thrust increases, corresponding changes in girls being less marked. Boys also show a marked improvement in their ability to run. It should be noted, however, that there may be a time lag between adolescent's growth spurt and strength spurt. The boy's strength is increasing all the time. But for a while he may have the stature of a man but a strength not yet appropriate to that of an adult. In these circumstances, however, it is scarcely true to say that he has 'outgrown his strength'. Again, it is commonly said that the adolescent is clumsy. This, too, is not strictly true, for the boy's muscular co-ordination increases most rapidly at the same time as his strength. His apparent clumsiness reflects that for a short while his muscular co-ordination is not as close to its maximum as his size is to its upper limit.

The performance of many girls in athletic events seems to diminish after 14 or 15 and it has been suggested that menarche signals the approximate end of the increase in strength for girls. This change in level of performance may, however, be because the motivation of girls in respect of athletic events or physical activities involving strength decreases in many girls in adolescence. But it is true that most girls have passed the peak performance in respect of physical skills by 18. Boys, however, have surpassed all but the most exceptional girls in respect of size, physical skill and strength by this age, and furthermore, they will go on improving in these respects.

Boys have also shown the trend to earlier maturation. And they, like the girls, show marked individual differences. Some boys and girls of 13 or 14 have reached sexual maturity and are approaching the strength and skill of the adult while others of the same chronological age are still children. This can cause serious psychological problems for the late developer, quite apart from the fact that our educational system tends to treat pupils at a given age as if they were all the same physiologically (124).

Skeletal age

The most useful index of physiological development is skeletal age. By means of skeletal analysis, the present status of bone formation is studied using X-rays. The calcium content within the ossified areas makes the latter opaque to such rays and renders them distinct from areas of cartilage where ossification has not yet commenced. In this way a bone age is obtained. In practice the hand or wrist bones are the ones studied although in theory any bone could be used. This technique has shown that there is a substantial positive correlation between skeletal and sexual maturation. It is possible also by counting the number of teeth erupted and relating these to standard figures, to obtain a dental age. According to Tanner (124) use may be made of the calcification of teeth, as indicated by X-rays of jaw, to give an index of dental maturity as skeletal age used stages of bone ossification.

Boys are, on the average, behind girls in skeletal age from birth onwards, as they are in dental maturity during the whole of permanent dentation eruption. It seems as if difference between the sexes in this respect is due to the action of genes located on the Y chromosome. At birth girls are almost four weeks ahead of boys in skeletal age, and from then until maturity their skeletal age is about 125 per cent of that of boys of the same chronological age. It is, of course, because of this that girls attain adolescence and adult stature some two years ahead of boys.

Growth and genetics

According to Tanner (124) identical and fraternal twin sisters reach menarche, on the average, about two and ten months apart respectively. For ordinary sisters the difference in time is greater. These data suggest that at least under conditions of life existing in Western Europe (or similar) much of the variability in the age of the onset of menarche is due to heredity. Indeed, it is considered that the age is determined by many genes contributing a small effect and that these are derived from the father as well as the mother. Skeletal age likewise shows close agreement in identical twins, and it is now thought that under normal conditions of life, physical development in general is under genetic control. Not all genes are active at birth; some exert their influence only under appropriate physiological conditions. So it seems that even the size and the timing of the adolescent growth spurt may be under genetic control.

Short periods of malnutrition appear to have few lasting effects on development. Growth slows until the diet is improved but children then catch up at closely the same rates in respect of skeletal age, height and weight and the final state is little different from that had there been no malnutrition. On the other hand chronic malnutrition certainly does slow down growth and results in diminished size. It is also of interest to note that boys are more easily thrown off their growth curves than are girls when affected by illness or malnutrition. In Tanner's view (124) this may well be due to the fact that the girl possesses two X chromosomes, since this sex difference is also in evidence in animals and in this case it is known that genetic factors are responsible for this regulation of growth in the face of adversity.

CONSTITUTION AND BEHAVIOUR

In this section there is a short discussion on the relationship between constitution and behaviour, the term 'constitution' including both heredity and the effects of all other influences which affect the individual's development. It is true, of course, that our knowledge in this general area is limited. The position is further complicated by the fact that heredity and environmental influences are correlated. Thus a child who is naturally intelligent is likely to be encouraged by parents and teachers and to receive a better schooling: again, a child who has an innate tendency to be introverted may receive less encouragement from people around him to join in social life.

Heredity and personality

Vandenburg (127) and Gottesman (45) have both shown that there are a number of personality traits which seem to be genetically determined to a considerable degree. For example, the tendency to be shy or bold, introverted or extroverted, and in the case of males to be dominant or submissive, is due in part to heredity. Teachers are particularly interested in the influences which determine a child's intelligence. Work involving studies of monozygotic and dizygotic twins clearly show that the capacity to become intelligent is determined to some extent by heredity (cf. Burt 20). Again, Burks (18) studied children who had been placed in foster homes before 12 months of age. The intelligence quotients of these children were compared with those of their foster parents, and it was found that the relationship was lower than it was when the intelligence quotients of children were compared with those of their biological parents. From these and other studies it is clear that the potentiality to be bright is influenced by the genotype. While the environment and opportunities are also important influences affecting the level of measured intelligence, it does seem that these influences work within limits, which may be wide, set by heredity. There is also some evidence that the X chromosome plays a role in determining the child's aptitude in respect of spatial visualisation, i.e. the ability to perceive, interpret and mentally rearrange objects spatially related. For example, Money (92) has shown that the IQ obtained on a verbal test is generally much higher than that obtained on a performance test in girls who have sex chromosome complement of XO (see later in this chapter).

Heredity and mental health

There are a few rare forms of mental illness which are clearly due to genetic causes, but there is much disagreement about the part heredity plays in the great majority of mental disorders. In the case of maladjustment and the neuroses – in the latter condition the person has some insight into his condition in the sense that he knows that not all is well – heredity does appear to play some part (114). It seems as if some children come into the world with a central nervous system less robust than that of others and succumb to maladjustment more easily when placed under psychological stress. It must be emphasised, however, that everyone can become maladjusted and suffer eventual breakdown if the stress is sufficiently intense and is experienced for long enough periods. The point is that some people break down more readily than others. Teachers only occasionally meet the more serious mental illnesses termed psychoses. In these, the individual loses contact with reality and there is far less insight into the condition of the self than is the case in the neuroses. There is certainly much dispute over the part played by heredity in these conditions. In some forms of psychoses it seems that heredity plays a major role; in others it appears that psychological and social factors in the environment, or physiological conditions within the individual are very important influences.

Effects of early maturity

There is much evidence that in some cultures, the early maturing male has many advantages over the late maturing one. The former is likely to be regarded by his peers as more physically attractive, more relaxed and more often chosen as leader in athletics and social events. Against this, late maturing boys are likely to feel dominated and rejected by their peers and generally feel inadequate. But it does seem likely that there is an interaction between early maturation and experience. The early maturer can be identified as being forward in development long before adolescence, and adults are likely to give him privileges and tasks normally reserved for chronologically older children. In similar manner late developers are likely to experience more childish treatment over a number of years. This they may resent but it may help to build their self pictures and shape their conduct, and they may well express their resentment in impulsive and rebellious behaviour. A comparative study of Italian and American boys (94) suggests that early maturing Italian boys have lower self concepts and less self confidence than early maturing American boys, suggesting that body development is more important as a means of identifying one's sex-role in the USA than in Italy. In some cultures, then, at least, the cards are stacked against the late maturing boy. Even if he is not adversely effected by the reactions of others to him, he may develop anxieties about his own masculinity and competence in sexual-social skills. At the same time it is important to appreciate that what has been said of the behavioural concomitants of early maturation is somewhat tentative, for our argument involved group trends and there are individuals who run counter to them.

Early maturation in the girl does not appear to have the same significance for her for neither physical acceleration nor retardation have shown themselves to be consistently advantageous. Nevertheless, some girls do suffer embarrassment when their breasts are developing and may show this embarrassment at times in the classroom and when changing for games or physical education.

Influence of parental and birth conditions on behaviour

During pregnancy the foetus may suffer damage as may the infant during actual childbirth. There may thus result an impairment of the central nervous system which may affect behaviour. Some workers take the view that in a proportion of these instances heredity plays a role in that the genetic make up renders the organism more or less vulnerable to particular stresses. In other instances it is clear that heredity is responsible for the impairment. However, there is now increasing evidence that the survivors of such damage (i.e. those who do not die) may show a range of disabilities extending from cerebral palsy, epilepsy and mental deficiency, through all types of behaviour problem and learning disabilities (95). Even the lesser degrees of damage may be enough to affect behaviour in some individuals since these may be less able, due to heredity, to tolerate stress. Furthermore, there is a great incidence of abnormal pregnancy and prematurity among persons in the lowest socio-economic groups for environmental conditions are less favourable and we find, as we should expect, a greater incidence of neuropsychiatric disorders, more delinquency and more maladjustment in these groups.

Stott (119, 120) has also put forward rather similar views. He speaks of an impairment of motivation brought about by damage or dysfunction of the neural structures. Either heredity, or adverse

B

effects during pregnancy or delivery, could impair both the physical development of the individual and the nervous system. The latter could result in more delinquency and maladjustment because of the individual's reduced capacity to handle stressful situations. Furthermore, Stott points out that the manner and extent of prenatal impairment depends on the genetic make-up of both mother and foetus. A genetic tendency to a particular malfunction may become manifest only under stress in pregnancy.

Variation in chromosome number

There are a number of abnormalities in which the cells do not contain the normal complement of chromosomes. The best-known example of this is, perhaps, that of mongolism, the incidence of which increases with the age of the mother. It has been shown that the condition results from errors in chromosome segregation. Most mongols have cells which contain an extra autosome (i.e. a non sex-determining chromosome) giving 47 chromosomes in all, although a small number of mongols have the normal number of chromosomes. In the more typical cases some environmental event seems likely to bring about the extra chromosome, although a genetic factor may be operating as well. In ovagenesis the egg cells are partially formed and they are retained in this state for many years, so that the ova of older mothers are likely to be exposed to the presumed external influence far longer than those of younger mothers. In the case of males, however, spermatogenesis involves the continuous production of gametes so there is no cumulative effect resulting from any environmental influences. In the case of those mongols whose cells have 46 chromosomes, there is, nevertheless, an error in chromosome segregation. Moreover, there exists the possibility that there is a gene responsible for the error in these instances. It is also possible that an inherited predisposition to error in chromosome segregation could also account for the presence of modified forms of some stigmata in relatives who are otherwise normal.

Variations in chromosomal sex-types

Not all individuals who are male in phenotype have an XY assortment of sex chromosomes. A few have an XXY chromosomal arrangement and not many of these individuals have complete sexual development and produce mature sperm. Likewise there are children who are girls in phenotype, but who possess a sex chromosome complement XO, i.e. one chromosome is missing. These individuals have limited development of the ovaries. Such pupils are encountered from time to time in school.

However, children with a chromosomal sex-type XXY have a skeletal development of normal boys (XY) and girls with an XO constitution show the earlier acceleration of growth of a normal girl (XX) suggesting, as stated earlier, that it is the genes carried on the Y chromosome which are responsible for the later adolescent growth spurt in boys. But there are individuals who have abnormal sexual development in the sense that the genotype and phenotype sex is inconsistent although they possess the normal complement of sex chromosomes. It seems likely that there are other environmental and heredity influences which can, at times, take precedence over the normal mechanism of sex determination and so it is necessary to distinguish between sex determination and sex differentiation.

MATURATION

Maturation plays an important role in human development and it is necessary to say what is meant by the term. The definition proposed is that given by Ausubel (5); namely, maturation consists of development that is attributable to genetic and/or incidental experience. Defined in this way maturation is not synonymous with development due to 'internal ripening', nor does it deny that environmental influences may play a role in maturation. But it does distinguish development which is mainly due to specific experience from development which is not.

In practice it is difficult to separate the effects of maturation from those of learning. Ausubel (5) has also usefully pointed out that the relative contributions of genetic factors, incidental experience, and specific practice to development, varies as between capacities or traits. In the case of those traits that are uniform for all human beings (phylogenetic traits), development is largely controlled by genetic factors (as in the case of human growth) and incidental experience plays a supportive role. At the other extreme are those traits that vary from culture to culture (psychosocial traits). In these genetic factors are of lesser importance, specific practice and experience are essential, while incidental experience may or may not be important. In between there are the many traits that show general uniformities in growth in all cultures but vary a great deal in respect of specific details of cultures or outcomes (psychobiological traits); e.g. intelligence. Here genetic factors play a marked role, incidental experience a very significant part, but specific practice is less important.

It can be seen that genetic and experimental factors are involved in maturation and in learning. Maturation is not the same as readiness – a term often used in education. Both maturation and learning are involved in a child's readiness to cope with a new experience.

NOTE

1. Height $= 0.7301 + 0.0437t + 0.2589 \log t$ when height is measured in cms and t in years.

FURTHER READING

Birch, H. G. and Lefford, A. 'Visual Differentiation, Intersensory Integration and Voluntary Motor Control,' *Monogr. Soc. Res. in Child Developm.*, **32** (2) (1967).

Carter, C.O. *Human Heredity* (London, Penguin 1962)

Cattell, R. B. *The Scientific Analysis of Personality*, chapter 2 (London, Penguin 1965)

Darlington, C. D. *Genetics and Man* (London, Penguin 1966)

Eichorn, D. H. In *Child Psychology*, chapter 1 (Chicago National Society for the Study of Education 1963)

Fuller, J. L. and Thompson, W. R. *Behaviour Genetics* (London, Wiley 1960)

Stott, L. H. *Child Development*, chapters 2, 3, 4, 5 (London, Holt, Rinehart and Winston 1967)

Tanner, J. M. *Growth at Adolescence*, 2nd ed. (Oxford, Blackwell 1962)

2 The Growth of Logical Thought

Introduction

In this context by the term 'thinking' we mean a connected flow of ideas or mental actions directed towards some clear end or purpose. Such a definition distinguishes between true thinking on the one hand, and dreams and day-dreams on the other. In fantasy, for example, our thoughts wander, are often unconnected, and are not consciously checked.

At the onset it is necessary to make clear why the growth of thought will be dealt with from the viewpoint of Piaget's developmental system. It does not seem to the writer that so complex an issue as the growth of structured thought can be explained in terms of what has traditionally been called learning theory, in spite of the valiant attempts on the part of, say, Staats and Staats (118) to account for complex human behaviour in this way. It is also possible to explain the growth of cognition, or knowing, using Bruner's (17) conceptual framework. In this the child makes information available to himself first through action in the earliest months and years of life, then through imagery, and finally through the symbolism of language. At the moment, however, there is little evidence that it offers teachers a more useful way of looking at the problem of intellectual growth than does the conceptual framework of Piaget. Bruner is correct to stress the importance, for the child, of translating concepts which have been derived through one way of representing the environment to himself (e.g. through action) into another way (e.g. through language). Nevertheless, the point of view regarding the growth of thought presented here is that of Piaget and his colleagues since their position seems to be of most help to teachers at present. At the same time, however, it must be stressed that his system is

[margin annotation: Bruner]

inadequate to explain all the facts and one day it will be replaced by, or subsumed under, a more all-embracing one.

SOME BASIC IDEAS IN PIAGET'S DEVELOPMENTAL SYSTEM

During his schoolboy days Piaget became a keen student of zoology, while in adolescence and early adulthood he became drawn to EPISTEMOLOGY, i.e. the theory or science of the method or ground of knowledge. His study of the writings of the French philosopher, Bergson, led him to believe that biology could serve his interest in epistemology, although he also realised that he needed a mediator between the two. Eventually he chose intelligence to play this role, and a series of studies on the growth of epistemology was the outcome. Moreover, in their efforts to bridge the gap between biology and epistemology, Piaget and his colleagues provided a volume of information and a wealth of detail of great value to teachers.

Piaget (102) starts from the point of view that as all organisms adapt to their environment, they must possess some form of structure or organisation which makes the adaptation possible at all. Thus he views ORGANISATION and ADAPTATION as the basic invariants of functioning. Moreover, since Piaget considers intellectual functioning as only a special case of general biological functioning, he regards organisation and adaptation as essential to the former as well. Furthermore, adaptation can be subdivided into two closely interwoven components ASSIMILATION and ACCOMMODATION. The former involves changing the elements in the situation (e.g. experience or food) so that they can be incorporated into the structure of the organism (e.g. the intellectual or digestive systems) in order that the organism may adapt to the situation. The latter term implies modifying the structure of the organism (e.g. in the intellectual or digestive systems) so that the organism can adapt to the situation. Assimilation and accommodation are thus regarded as functional invariants as well. Thus for Piaget every intellectual act necessitates some intellectual structure, while intellectual functioning is characterised by assimilation and accommodation.

As the baby interacts with his environment he builds up sequences of actions, or patterns of behaviour which have definite structure, called SCHEMAS. In the post infancy period the term schema refers to mental actions and intellectual structures. Thus in the first days of life Piaget speaks of the schema of sucking; in adolescence, of the schema of proportion. In assimilation the child has to absorb new experiences into his existing schemas, whereas in accommodation there is the modification of existing schemas or the build up of new ones. But once new experience is assimilated the child's schemas become more complex, and because of this, accommodations of even greater complexity are possible.

Piaget's observations led him to believe that children repeat playfully and with seeming pleasure those schemas that are in the process of organisation. When such schemas have become organised, the apparent pleasure disappears and the schemas cease to be repeated unless they are combined to form more complex schemas or serve as a means to some end. It is because one of the essential properties of a schema is its need for further interaction with the environment, thereby perfecting the schema itself or allowing it to become incorporated within a wider schema, that the main source of motivation comes from within the young child. The level of this intrinsic motivation does, of course, vary from child to child, due perhaps to the level of activity in certain areas of the central nervous system. But when schemas required for the solution to some problem are not too far removed in complexity from those available to the child, the inadequacies of existing schemas force him to accommodate to the conditions of the problem, thereby extending the capacity for further learning. Again, in Piaget's view, schemas do not remain unchanged even in the absence of environmental stimulation; they are constantly reorganised and linked with others, so that meanings become linked with wider meanings. Even so the growth of intelligence is slow. Nevertheless, changes in the schemas brought about by attempts at accommodation, and reorganisations brought about independent of external stimulation, together ensure schemas of greater complexity and hence intellectual growth.

Piaget (100) has provided much evidence to suggest that there is a fixed sequence of stages in the growth of thought, and that thinking at one stage is qualitatively different from that at another. It is true that the age at which children reach the varying stages varies because of their educational and cultural backgrounds, the degree of intellectual stimulation they receive, and heredity. Nevertheless the sequence or pattern is there, and it is to a consideration of these stages that we now turn.

SENSORI-MOTOR PERIOD

The normal baby comes into the world possessing a number of REFLEX-like capacities which are innate; for example, he cries, moves his tongue, sucks and so on. But at first he does this only in response to an appropriate stimulus from without. However, before the end of the first month he begins to experiment by 'trial and error' and so is led, for example, to discriminate between the things that are suckable from those that are not. This tendency to suck extends to cot blanket, rattle or anything else within his reach. It is in these very early acts of discrimination that the *origins* of thinking are located. Between the ages of one and four months we get the next sub-stage of babyhood. The infant, happening upon some action by chance, repeats it for its own sake; for example, there is repetitive opening and closing of fists or fingering of blanket. Here Piaget introduces the idea of PRIMARY CIRCULAR REACTION to indicate that the baby repeats the new chance adaptation again and again. Moreover, there is the beginning of coordination between one action and another. For example, coordination of hand and arm permits thumb sucking, while by the end of the stage the infant tries to look at whatever he happens to grasp and he tries to grasp whatever he sees.

At this point the child moves forward to the third sub-stage of the sensori-motor period which lasts from about five to eight months of age. He now shows behaviour patterns which Piaget calls SECONDARY CIRCULAR REACTIONS, the essence of these being the child's attempts to maintain, through repetition, interesting changes brought about in the environment – external to his body – which were first produced by chance. For example, the baby may accidentally touch a swinging rattle and the action of grasping and shaking the rattle is then repeated as a whole. Moreover he now begins to show evidence of being able to differentiate the means by which he brought the end about – the arm movement – from the end itself, i.e. shaking the rattle; at least after the event. He thus begins to show some small anticipation of his own actions and hence the onset of intention. There thus originates in elementary form the capacity to behave in a purposive way. Between the ninth and the end of the twelfth month the infant shows behaviour characteristic of the next substage. Coordination has now reached the point where he can set aside an obstacle to reach a desired object, and he can use an object to attain a goal. For example, he will seize a handkerchief hiding an object and retrieve the latter; and he will take an adult's fingers and place them on his own to perform some task which he cannot execute on his own.

Sub-stage five lasts until the child is around eighteen months old. It is the period during which the TERTIARY CIRCULAR REACTION appears. Whereas in the case of the secondary circular reaction the child has only the vaguest notion of a relationship between his behaviour and the result – the behaviour schemas are repeatedly activated but in a mechanical way – in the case of the tertiary circular reaction, there is evidence of the child experimenting really to explore the situation. There is the attempt to pursue the novel and to assimilate those features of the situation which are not quite assimilable to the schemas available. Thus, as a result of a sort of experimentation in the search for something fresh, new schemas are established. Thus the baby will let an object fall to the floor to see what happens; he will knock objects, shake them, and throw them to see if they will roll or bounce. New ways of doing things are discovered based on an understanding of new relationships so that the infant will pull a box to himself to get a doll placed on it but which was otherwise out of reach.

The last of the sub-stages is found around eighteen to twenty-one months or so. When the infant is faced with a new situation for which he has no schema available, overt trial and error is no longer as necessary as it was earlier to attain the desired end. In simple situations the awareness of relationships is now sufficiently developed that he can invent new means, and see which actions will succeed and which will not, without actually putting them to the test. This invention comes through a covert process that amounts to inner or mental experimentation for the infant can increasingly represent to himself the various possible actions and how they must be combined, in order to attain some desired end. His actions are carried out in inward form; he has a flow of ideas directed to some end or purpose. In short, actions have become internalised and he is beginning to think. The first twenty-one months or so of life is called by Piaget the period of sensori-motor intelligence, the schemas built up during this period needing the direct support of information obtained through the senses and through motor action. Each element in the schema comes into being at the exact moment when other aspects of the environment provide the necessary support for it.

So far we have described the overall characteristics of the development of sensori-motor intelligence. At the same time there is the growth of the more specialised intellectual achievements; i.e., the sensori-motor construction of causality, imitation, objects, play, space and time. Indeed, it is during this period that the basic schemas are elaborated for dealing with the environment as, for example, in the case of space when the child adjusts his actions to reach near and distant objects, and in the case of time when he adjusts his actions to catch a swinging rattle.

PRE-OPERATIONAL THOUGHT

For Piaget the child moves out of the stage of sensori-motor intelligence into what he calls the pre-operational stage of thought when he can differentiate a signifier (e.g. image, word) from a significate, i.e. what it is the signifier stands for, and call forth the one to represent the other. The capacity to make this differentiation and to be able to make an act of reference is termed the SYMBOLIC FUNCTION by Piaget.

During the sensori-motor period when a child can execute a movement he tends, if he sees an analogous movement in another person or object, to assimilate it to his own. So for Piaget, imagery, in evidence from about 12 months of age, is in essence internalised imitation. Exactly how this comes about is unknown, but it is plausible that imagery is aided by the over practice of the motor act. Imagery is thus the child's first signifier, and examples of the use of imagery in representing situations to himself can be readily seen in his everyday play. This kind of signifier is termed a symbol signifier by Piaget because such are more or less private signifiers which bear some physical resemblance to their referents. Later the child can use language so that he can use the word 'horse' to stand for, or represent, the animal and talk about it in its absence. For Piaget, language is a sign signifier, for it is socially shared.

With the onset of language the nature of the child's intelligence greatly changes. Representational thought can grasp a number of events as a coherent whole, whereas at the level of sensori-motor intelligence successive actions and perceptual states are linked one by one. Moreover, representational thought provides the child with a less transient and far more flexible model of the outside world, and extends the range of thought well outside the present environment for he is no longer dependent on action and immediate perception for thought. The onset of language is also important in other ways although it is not the place to discuss this here: for example, the increased use of language gradually changes the child's relationships with his family for the increased communication makes easier the socialisation of the child. However, it is important to note that for Piaget thought comes before language, the latter is fitted on to the former, and while a socially shared linguistic system may play some part in the growth of thought, it is quite inadequate to explain the origins of the latter.

Between 2 and 4 years of age intellectual development seems to consist largely in the building up of this representational activity, and in differentiating the image and language on the one hand, from action and reality on the other. All that was performed at the sensori-motor stage now has to be reworked, as it were, using language. Indeed, there seems to be slow progress during these years in problem solving apart from those due to physical development and the growth of manipulative skills. Many items in intelligence tests for this age range involve the child's comprehension of verbal instructions; drawing – which is a form of representation – and copying a given model. This period, from 2 to 4 years, is also termed the preconceptual stage by Piaget, and the notions which the child builds up are termed preconcepts. At this age the child cannot grasp the concept of a class of objects, e.g. class of dogs. He cannot decide if, say, the 'wind' made by a fan is the same object as the breeze that blows the leaves or two distinct terms that belong to the same class. The child is now at the first level of abstraction or dissociation, for he dissociates objects and their properties on the basis of their behaviour; e.g. knife that cuts bread from knife that cuts apples. Again there is much transductive reasoning, or reasoning from particular to particular at this stage. The child will argue that as mummy is combing her hair she must be going out because she combed her hair before she went out before. While this kind of reasoning gives the correct answer at times, on other occasions it obviously leads the child into the grossest errors.

Around the fourth birthday we see a change beginning in the child's intellectual growth. Between then and about $5\frac{1}{2}$ years of age he is more able to examine and set about a specific task, adapt his intelligence to it, and commence to reason about more difficult everyday problems. Even so, one of the marked characteristics of thought at this stage is its tendency to *centre*, as Piaget terms it, on some striking feature of the object about which he is reasoning to the exclusion of other relevant aspects, with the result that the reasoning is distorted. If two similar bottles of lemonade have their respective contents emptied into two glasses of very different shape, so that the heights of the lemonade are markedly different, the 4-year-old will deny that the amounts of lemonade in the glasses are the same. The child seems unable to take into account two contrasting features (height and width in this case) which could balance and thus compensate for the distortion brought about by concentrating on one aspect of the situation. In short the child is unable to *decentre*. Again, pre-operational thought tends to focus on successive states in a situation or display rather than on the transformations which changed one state into another (as in the case of the lemonade); it is irreversible in that the child is unable to move back, in his mind, to the starting point from which his thinking began; and the child at this stage of thought is incapable of seeing a situation from other than a personal point of view. In brief, he is egocentric. However, around 5½ years of age the rigid and irreversible intellectual structures begin to become more flexible and there is a transition to the next stage of thought. Piaget calls the overall 4- to 7-year-old period one of intuitive thought. In this case the term intuition indicates the rather isolated and sporadic actions in the mind which occasionally give a foretaste of later systematised thinking, but which do not yet coalesce into an integrated system of thought as they do when operational thought sets in around 7 to 8 years of age.

CONCRETE OPERATIONAL THOUGHT

Consider again the two bottles of lemonade that the child agrees contain the same amount of liquid. When the contents are poured into glasses of varying shape so that the heights and surface areas of the liquids are markedly different, the 5-year-old is likely to deny that the amounts of lemonade are equal. At 6 he may agree to equality in some instances but deny it in others, depending on the shape of the glasses and the perceptual differences involved. But at 7 to 8 years of age the child maintains the equality of the amounts of lemonade whatever the size and shape of the vessels. He will reply, 'You've only poured it'; or 'You haven't added any or taken any away'. He realises now that, say, 'short wide' can be changed into 'tall narrow' and vice versa; that is, he now envisages complete and reversible compensations. Thought has now become what adults call systematised, logical, or internally consistent, and the child has reached what Piaget terms the stage of concrete operational thought or first order operational schemas.

An entirely different but very important example to illustrate the growth of logical thought is to be found in the child's ability to classify objects. Suppose that objects can be classified in terms of three colours, three shapes and three sizes. The 6-year-old may well group the objects on the basis of a common attribute, say, shape, and then subdivide the three groups (rectangles, squares, circles) into sub-groups. But the rectangles may be formed into sub-groups on the basis of, say, colour and each colour further divided on the basis of size, while the square and circle sub-groups may be sorted on the basis of size and each size further divided by colour. This is what Piaget calls a collection and not a true classification. In a true classification, which occurs around 7 to 8 years of age, the groups are further sorted on the basis of colour or size consistently and subjects keep in mind the inclusion relationship which obtains between a class and its sub-class. Moreover, in a true classification the child can switch to making his first groupings on the basis of, say, colour and then sub-divide consistently on the basis of size or shape. True classification thus depends on the child's ability to identify clearly the criteria upon which the classification is made.

At 7 to 8 the schemas which have developed are altogether different in kind from those present at 4 to 5 years of age. The capacity to reason and understand demands a higher order schema which permits a simultaneous grasp of successive sequences in the mind. The child can now look on in his own thinking and monitor it; in short he is aware of the sequences of action in his mind. Moreover, for any action in his mind he can now understand that there are other actions that will give the same result. In other words he can appreciate equivalences between transformations that come as a result of the anticipation of virtual actions and their effects. Thus the child understands that $2+3 = 4+1 = 8-3$; or that the same distance can be measured in feet and inches and that the figures will mean the same thing; or that subtraction can be performed using complementary addition. Furthermore, as we saw in the last paragraph, it is now possible for the child to distinguish between his experiences and the order that he imposes on these experiences. In brief he has now reached the second level of abstraction or dissociation.

There is now learning with understanding. At the level of sensori-motor and pre-operational thought there was a great deal of learning, but little or no understanding in that the child learned a linear series of actions at a level at which it does not seem possible to elaborate a set of equivalences between transformations. One must not belittle learning that takes place before thought becomes systematic, for such learning is essential to the growth of logical thought itself.

In Piaget's system the term 'action' is a generic one. In the sensori-motor period, actions are generally observable as when the child moves one object to find another. Later, actions become increasingly internalised as we have seen; they become more mobile and they increasingly cohere to form complex and integrated systems of actions. When such mental actions have a definite and strong structure, they are termed by Piaget OPERATIONS. Thus any action which is an integral part of an organised network of related actions is an operation. Hence, in Piaget's view, concrete operational thought must possess certain properties and unless these are present thought will show inconsistencies. These properties are:

1. Closure. Any two operations can be combined to form a third operation. E.g., $4+5=9$; all men plus all women equals all adults.

2. Reversibility. For any operation there is an opposite operation which cancels it. E.g. $4+5=9$ and $9-5=4$; all men plus all women equals all adults, but all adults except all men equals all women.

3. Associativity. When three operations are combined it does not matter which two are combined first; or the same goal can be reached by different routes. E.g. $(2+1)+3 = 2+(1+3)$; all men plus all women plus all children equals all women plus all children plus all men.

4. Identity. This is the 'null operation', and is performed when any operation is combined with its opposite.

It is, however, important to stress that at this stage the child's logical thought extends only to objects and events of first hand reality.

Because the child can now see the part he plays in ordering his experience and he can identify the ways in which he does this, he can build a new kind of notion. Such are termed concepts by Piaget, as distinct from the pre-concept of the 3-year-old, and they are built at the second level of abstraction or dissociation. We have already seen that the child can classify; he can also build a series, and grasp the concept of the natural numbers (the numerosity of sets). Moreover, as he moves up through the primary school his thinking shows more and more flexibility of operational manipulation of the first order relationships and reasoning can be extended to greater areas of his experience. Thus he becomes able to build the concepts of length, weight, time, area, etc. (although not all at the same time) and the world becomes a more meaningful place to live in. It is not possible to dwell on the great amount of work that has been done on the growth of concept formation and logical thought generally (cf. Flavell (38); Lovell (77); Wallace (132)) although it must be stressed that the development of systemised thinking is a slow process. Laurendeau and Pinard (70) have shown that realism or egocentrism – regarding one's own perspective as immediately objective and absolute – persists on and off until around $6\frac{1}{2}$ years of age; and artificialism – the positing of explicit action of a maker at the origin of things – does not disappear until 9. Furthermore, they found that animism – the giving of life and consciousness to surrounding objects – still persists occasionally up to 11 or 12 years of age. This clearly illustrates that the extension of systematised thought to diverse fields of experience is slow.

FORMAL OPERATIONAL THOUGHT

From 11 to 12 onwards in the ablest pupils, and from 13 to 14 in ordinary children, new thinking skills begin to emerge. As the child becomes better at organising and structuring data with the methods of concrete operational thought, he becomes aware that such methods do not lead to a logically exhaustive solution to his problems. For example, he may find that most light objects float, but at times the rule is transgressed as when he finds that some heavy objects float and some light objects sink. He gropes for new methods of attack, often in Piaget's view (Inhelder and Piaget (60)) as the adolescent commits himself to real life situations. Due to the maturation of the central nervous system and, even more important, due to the continued interaction with the cultural milieu (particularly in the case of the more developed societies) together with the resulting feedback, the individual can now produce more complex expectations when faced with certain kinds of data or situations. The schemas are again new in kind and the adolescent has reached the stage of formal operational thought. Whereas the junior school child can make some extension of the actual in the direction of the possible, the adolescent can set up a number of hypotheses and establish which are compatible with the evidence in front of him. In short, he can invert reality and possibility, and look upon the facts in front of him as the sub set of a set of possible transformations that have actually come to pass. The essence of formal thought is as Lunzer (83) has argued, the ability of the pupil to elaborate second order relationships, i.e. the ability to structure and co-ordinate actions upon first order relations which themselves result from the coordination of actions upon objects. This is in complete agreement with Piaget's own views for Inhelder and Piaget write (60 p. 254), 'Obviously this notion of second degree operations also expresses the general characteristic of formal thought – it goes beyond the framework of transformations bearing directly on empirical reality (first degree operations) and subordinates it to a system of hypothetico-deductive operations, that is, operations which are possible.'

A familiar experiment to test the pupil's capacity to build himself a system of hypothetico-deductive operations is that involving a simple pendulum. He is given a length of string suspended from a hook, together with one of a number of weights which can be attached at the lower end, and he is asked to establish what it is that determines the length of the swing. The subject can vary the length of the string, the weight used for the bob, the height from which the bob is released, and the impetus he gives to it. The correct solution can only be reached if the young person reasons that if a particular variable, say, the length of string, determines the period of swing, then the expected effect will occur if he holds all the other variables constant and varies only the one he is considering. Conversely, if he does this and finds the period of swing remains unaffected, he must infer that the length of string is not a relevant variable. Up to 13 or 14 years of age subjects do not understand the necessity of holding the other variables constant, although younger pupils can sometimes be led to understand the 'method of all other things equal' while not

c

adopting it spontaneously. Because the adolescent can manipulate statements dealing with possibilities, in systematic fashion, he can for any set of transformations see a greater range of equivalent transformations compared with the junior school child.

It must be stressed that formal operational thought is applicable in all areas of the curriculum and not just in science and technology. In a study carried out under the writer's direction (Hallam, 49) dealing with thinking in relation to historical questions, it was clearly demonstrated that the replies were at the stage of pre-operational, concrete operational and formal operational thought. Indeed, formal thought comes late in respect of historical thinking.

With the coming of the ability to elaborate second order relations the adolescent is able to build an entirely new kind of concept. Take for example the schema of proportion. An analogy of the form 3 : 7 as 15 : 35 involves a certain relationship between the first two terms, a certain relationship between the second pair of terms, and the establishment of an identity relationship between these two relationships. The logical structure of such a system is exactly parallel to that of a statement of proportionality. There is much experimental evidence (cf. Lovell, 79) quite apart from the experience of the classroom, that proportion is understood at around 14 to 15 years of age. Outstandingly able pupils may grasp it at 12; the duller children never.

When the adolescent can build second order relations he is ready to elaborate many of the important concepts used in science and technology. He can now build the concepts of, say, kinetic energy, heat, momentum. If we skip over the difficulty of equating weight and mass, we can say that mass and temperature are elaborated at the stage of concrete operational thought for these were derivable from first hand experience. But their product is not; it is a result of coordinating first order relationships. Heat as a concept does not become available until about 14 years of age onwards, although it is hoped that the teacher will help the child to acquire an intuitive notion of heat some years earlier. Moreover, before concepts can be derived at this the third level of abstraction, concepts derived at the second level of abstraction in the junior school have to be completely divorced from their concrete contexts and manipulated as 'pure' terms in the mind.

Piaget (60) argues that the age of onset of formal thought is relative to the culture pattern for in some undeveloped societies adolescents do not appear to attain this level of thought. So beyond some minimum age perhaps set by neurophysiological factors, the level of an individual's thinking may be a product of the progressive acceleration of individual development under the influence of education and culture. In developed societies particularly, the individual thinks beyond the present, this thinking being likely to be determined by the climate of opinion and expectancy in the community; the concepts made use of in that society; the experiences received at home, school, and work; and his social attitudes. But a proportion of individuals in such societies do not reach the stage of thought or reach it only now and again in familiar situations. What this proportion is, is not known. However, Peluffo's (97) study, which compared children born in Sardinia but who had lived in Genoa for varying lengths of time, with children born and brought up in Genoa, gives some indication of the likely effects of the culture pattern on the growth of formal thought.

SOME LIMITATIONS OF PIAGET'S SYSTEM

It is impossible in a book of this size to discuss, at length, the many weaknesses in the Piagetian system. For example, one frequent criticism is that Piaget sees more structure and system in the child's thought than is in fact there. Moreover our text might suggest that the growth of concrete and formal operational thought proceeds smoothly, and once these modes of thought are available they are applicable in all areas of experience simultaneously. In fact this is not so. It has frequently been shown both at the stage of concrete operational thought (cf. Dodwell, 26) and formal operational thought (cf. Lovell, 76) that there is only a moderate correlation between tests which involve the same intellectual structures. In the view of Inhelder and Piaget, thought is systematised in relation to length before it is in relation to weight, because it is more difficult to serialise, equalise, etc., objects whose properties are less easy to dissociate from one's actions (weight), than to apply mental operations to properties that can be rendered more objective (length). Thus at the level of concrete operational thought these horizontal age discrepancies are held to be contingent on intuitable or perceptual features of the situation. Such an explanation is not, however, possible at the stage of formal operational thought. The 'horizontal discrepancies' do not invalidate Piaget's analyses of the differences in structure between stages of thought, but it does limit Piagetian theory as a predictive and explanatory instrument.

Another major weakness is that we know too little about the processes underlying the movement from one stage of thought to the next. Piaget makes great use of the term EQUILIBRIUM. An important characteristic of a system in psychological equilibrium is its capacity to cancel or compensate perturbations which tend to change the existing state of equilibrium. When this state of equilibrium obtains in intellectual functioning there is a balance of assimilation and accommodation. The former process organises, directs and checks accommodations to reality, while assimilation itself is prevented from getting out of hand and becoming completely AUTISTIC through a lack of accommodation to the real world. Moreover, the mechanism which in Piaget's view is the propellent for the movement from one stage of intellectual development to the next is an equilibration process; i.e. this process of bringing assimilation and accommodation into balanced coordination. There is thus a constant development of lesser equilibrated schemes into better equilibrated ones. For example, concrete operational structures become integrated into formal operational structures, the latter being better equilibrated than the former. The real difficulty is in specifying precisely how these progressively better equilibrated states are brought about.

Piaget reports an experiment in which pupils between 5 and 8 years of age were shown a series of ten sticks ranging from 9 to 15 cms. in length and told to look at them. When asked to draw them a week later their efforts reflected the schematic level (complexity of schema) of the children. The youngest pupils drew pairs of sticks equal in length to one another, or groups of three also of equal length. At the stage of trial and error children drew 5 or 6 sticks varying in length. The older pupils at the level of concrete operational thought completed a series of from 9 to 12 sticks. Six months later they were asked to draw what they remembered, although in the meantime they had not seen the model again nor had they had any practice in forming a series in school. In 80 per cent of instances the second drawing showed progress over the first. The improvement in memory was due to the spontaneous development of schemas brought about by numerous activities and experiences of the child in the intervening period. This in Piaget's view is a clear example of interiorisation of actions and progressive equilibration leading up to concrete operational thinking.

In his view, early learning by trial and error is nothing more than the progressive construction of a schema by means of successive REGULATIONS, i.e. partial and momentary compensations which are midway between irreversible centrations and rigorously reversible operations. Thus each action modifies a subsequent action in a positive or negative way. Indeed, Piaget's hypothesis is that all sensori-motor experience resulting in schema development gives rise to regulations, which in the first instance explains the growth of schematisation itself. Thus there is a circular relationship as it were between schema and regulation. The schema makes possible the regulation, while the latter allows the growth of new and more complex schemas. Moreover the growth of the regulatory mechanisms permits the pre-correction of errors (i.e. before they are committed) and eventually the regulations give way to intellectual operations. The operation is thus a superior form of regulation in which approximate retro-actions (i.e. the processes whereby an individual revises earlier actions in the light of those that follow) give place to complete reversibility. Hence for Piaget, feedback plays an important role in the conversion of schemas of action into interiorised reversible operations. It is also his view that the child's ability to cancel through complete reversibility, and to compensate through considering two dimensions at once, underlies the latter's ability to solve the conservation problems. Whether or not the conservation tasks are in fact solved in this way must also await future research.

FACTORS INFLUENCING INTELLECTUAL GROWTH

For Piaget there are four major influences affecting intellectual growth. These may be briefly listed as follows:

1. Biological factors (e.g. maturation of the central nervous system) which probably determine the unfolding of the stages of such growth in a fixed sequence.
2. Equilibration or autoregulation factors. These intervening autoregulating factors are very important and, as we saw above, they probably lie at the origin of mental operations themselves, especially logical-mathematical operations.
3. General factors resulting from socialisation. These arise through exchanges, discussions, agreements and oppositions in social intercourse between children or between children and adults. Such influences operate to a greater or lesser extent in all cultures and they are closely linked to factor (2) since the general coordination of actions concern the inter-individual as well as the intra-individual.
4. Factors related to educational and cultural transmission. Such differ greatly from one society to another.

FURTHER READING

Almy, M. *Young Children's Thinking* (New York, Teachers College Press, Columbia University 1966)

Baldwin, A. L. *Theories of Child Development*, chapters 5-9 (London, Wiley 1967)

Brearley, M. and Hitchfield, E. *A Teacher's Guide to Reading Piaget* (London, Routledge and Kegan Paul 1966)

Bruner, J. S. *Studies in Cognitive Growth* (London, Wiley 1960)

Flavell, J. H. *The Developmental Psychology of Jean Piaget* (London, Van Nostrand 1963)

Inhelder, B. and Piaget, J. *The Early Growth of Logic in the Child* (London, Routledge and Kegan Paul 1964)

Klausmeier, H. J. and Harris, C. W. (Eds.) *Analysis of Concept Learning*, chapters 7, 13 (London, Academic Press 1966)

Lovell, K. 'Systematisation of Thought', *Development in Learning* 2 (Eds. Lunzer, E. A. and Morris, J. F.) (London, Staples 1968)

Lunzer, E. A. 'Formal Reasoning', *Development in Learning* 2 (Eds. Lunzer, E. A. and Morris, J. F.) (London, Staples 1968)

Maier, H. W. *Three Theories of Child Development*, chapter 3 (New York, Harper Row 1965)

Peel, E. A. *The Pupil's Thinking* (London, Oldbourne 1960)

Peluffo, N. 'Culture and Cognitive Problems', *Int. J. Psychol.*, 2, 187–98 (1967)

Piaget, J. *The Child's Conception of Number* (London, Routledge and Kegan Paul 1952)

Piaget, J. and Szemiska, A. *The Child's Conception of Geometry* (London, Routledge and Kegan Paul 1960)

Sigel, I. E. and Hooper, F. H. (Eds.) *Logical Thinking in Children* (London, Holt, Rinehart and Winston 1968)

Smedslund, J. 'Concrete Reasoning: A Study of Intellectual Development', *Monogr. Soc. Res. Child Developm.*, 29 (2) (1964)

Stott, L. H. *Child Development*, chapters 6, 10 (London, Holt, Rinehart and Winston 1967)

Thomson, R. *The Psychology of Thinking*, chapters 4–7 (London, Penguin 1959)

3 Some Aspects of the Growth of Perception

Introduction

Drever (29) defines PERCEPTION as the process of becoming immediately aware of something. The term is usually employed of sense perception when the thing of which we suddenly become aware is the object affecting a sense organ. Other workers have used the term perception in a rather wider fashion to include the recognition and identification of an object. On this view, perception is sensory awareness affected by the person's mental set, attitudes, expectations, motivation and general ways of thinking. For Piaget, perception certainly covers more than mere raw sensation, although he does not go as far as some others in respect of the wider view. He writes (101): 'We will call perception the most direct or immediate possible knowledge of a present object in the sensorial field (without affirming, however, that there exists a knowledge which is completely direct or immediate)'. It must be appreciated, however, that much research in perception has not dealt with awareness of the stimulation of the senses as such, but with the observable responses that accompany or follow such stimulation. Thus the scientist may have great difficulty in assessing directly a person's awareness of 'redness', but he can assess, say, how quickly the driver applies his brakes when the lights turn to red.

In this chapter a very rigorous selection of the available knowledge in this field of perception has had to be carried out and it will deal mainly, but not exclusively, with visual perception. However, an attempt has been made to highlight some of the basic issues relating to perception and human development which are of relevance to teachers, since the immediate role of perception is not always obvious to them. It is, of course, clear that perception is fundamental to human living. Before we can recognise anybody or anything, or have any sort of reaction to an object, we have first to be involved in one or more of the following: hearing, seeing, smelling, tasting, touching. Again it is obvious that perception is dependent on the growth and integrity of the central nervous system. Yet in spite of its importance and the great amount of research carried out, there is, as yet, no satisfactory theory to embrace all aspects of perception.

It is not intended to become involved in many of the arguments that have raged around the nature of perception. It is sufficient to say that the older views may be divided into two broad schools of thought. One – that of the empiricists – held that all knowledge comes through experience. The baby's mind is a blank or empty state at birth and learning results from perceiving. On this view perception is explained roughly as follows. Each stimulus received from the outside world is recorded by the mind, and when the same stimulus is received again on a subsequent occasion, the mind again makes reference to the original recording. On this view perception – regarded as a basic function of the mind – is in essence a passive activity. The second of the older views on the nature of perception was provided by the nativistic school of thought. This proposed, in effect, that the mechanisms of perception exist prior to experience; that is, they are inborn. On this view the way in which we perceive, say, space is inherited.

In an introductory text such as this it is impossible to review either the classical views on, or modern theories of, perception in any detail for the position is a complex one, and interested readers should consult Allport (1); also Pronko, Ebert and Greenberg (105). One of the important yet undecided issues is the part that motor action plays in the growth of perception. Both empiricists and nativists believed that action came before perception and permitted the development of the latter. Among contemporary views on perception Hebb (52) has expressed the view that it is learning which is based on repeated sequences of eye movements which underlies the growth of the perception of form, while for Piaget action becomes changed into perception and cognition through a complex series of stages in which experience at the sensori-motor stage plays a great part. Opposed to this general viewpoint are the views of Fantz (35). He maintains that perception comes before action and that early perceptual experience is essential for the growth of coordinated and visually directed behaviour, for example, following a swinging rattle; although improvement in motor coordination will certainly increase the efficiency of the perceptual processes. Indeed, so important are the theoretical positions of Fantz and Piaget that they are elaborated below.

Meanwhile it should be noted that many studies in the growth of perception in children have described stages through which children pass. These provide very useful information but in themselves they throw little light on the mechanisms which relate to why development occurs as it does. A second snag which has detracted from the value of some studies is that psychologists have not always defined their terms as rigorously as they ought so that the word, say, 'brightness' is unambiguous in its meaning. Some of the discrepant findings are due to this lack of clarity in definition. A third point to note is that perception cannot be tested completely independent of action. Even in the early weeks of life, the experimenter has to take the time spent by a baby looking at, say, one colour or pattern rather than another in order to study the child's visual preferences and hence his perceptual development.

THE POSITION OF R. L. FANTZ

R. L. Fantz is a recent but important worker in the field of perception and has provided a theoretical point of view. He distinguishes between two aspects of perception: viz. discrimination (what is it?) and localisation (where is it?). A single look or touch may, for the adult, give the required information on both these aspects, yet a baby may be able to follow a dangling ring with his eyes and yet may not be able to distinguish it from another ring. The contention of Fantz is that pattern discrimination is present at birth and is not dependent upon prior experience.

To support this viewpoint he has provided much evidence regarding pattern discrimination in babies right from birth, for infants seem to attend more to patterns than they do to either brightness or colour alone. Fantz (34) studied the reactions of children aged 1 to 15 weeks to pairs of patterns of varying complexity. At all ages they looked longest at complex pairs of patterns, viz. bull's eyes and horizontal stripes; next longest at two patterns of intermediate complexity, viz. circle v. cross and checks v. square; and least time at a control pair of identical triangles. In another experiment Fantz et al. (36) studied the development of visual acuity in infants. The finest or thinnest stripes that could be discriminated during the first eight weeks of life and under rather poor illumination, subtended 40 minutes of arc. This figure decreased to 10 minutes of arc in infants over sixteen weeks compared with 1 minute of arc for average adults. Again, under conditions of moderate illumination (which gave better results than either poor or bright conditions) stripes $\frac{1}{64}$ inch wide could be seen at a distance of some 15 inches by children at about three months of age. From this study it was concluded that the various aspects of the visual system are functioning, at least to some degree, soon after birth. In other studies Fantz (34, 35) has shown that both infants under five days old and infants between two and six months show far greater attention to a white face with black features than they do to, say, coloured discs. He has argued that the unlearned attention value of pattern compared with other visual stimuli is in agreement with other known facts regarding the structure and functioning of the visual system.

From his many studies, Fantz concludes that babies can, from birth, discriminate patterns as the basis for form perception, although not as well as adults can. In general, they tend to select and attend to complex patterns in preference to plain ones. Thus the infant is helped, right from the first days of life, to gain increased experience with certain aspects of the environment. But by the third month of life, at the latest, past experience is modifying the unlearned visual selectiveness, and thereafter there is an increased attention to novel patterns and a decreased attention to familiar ones. So the effects of early visual experiences help the infant by preparing him for a more active exploration of the environment. For Fantz, visual perception is certainly prior to action. At birth a simple form of perception is present but at that early stage the only visually directed response, that is, looking at something, is brought about and maintained by what is perceived. But with the developments that take place in the visual system and with the growth of various forms of sensori-motor coordination, perception is enabled to direct more active forms of behaviour. Furthermore the feedback and reinforcement from past responses may change what is attended to and perceived or they may change the nature of the response to what is perceived. At the same time, however, what is attended to and perceived influences, right from birth, both the child's actions and what is learnt from past actions.

THE VIEWS OF J. PIAGET

Piaget and his colleagues have carried out many experimental studies in the field of perception and he, too, has provided a theoretical framework inside which perception may be considered (see Vurpillot 129, Wohlwill 139). For him, perception is, like intelligence, a means by which the child adapts to his environment. But in his view the development of perception is dependent on the growth of sensori-motor intelligence in the first 21 to 24 months of life so that the child's early perceptions only have meaning for him through the growth of sensori-motor schemas of which they form a part. Later intellectual growth depends on sensori-motor intelligence and Piaget does not admit that intellectual growth is dependent on prior percepts although he does allow some interaction between the growth of intelligence and perception, as will be shown later. It can thus be seen that Fantz and Piaget disagree on some important issues. Piaget has also written a good deal on the differences between perception and intelligence from a structural point of view. In his view there are a number of perceptual phenomena which can be regarded as primitive forerunners of better structured intellectual phenomena which will develop later. He makes out a case for perceptual structures being semi-reversible, and while such structures can never have the complete manoeuvrability of concrete operational structures they are nevertheless partially ISOMORPHIC to the latter. Thus both developmentally and structurally perception is inferior to intelligence as a form of adaptation. It is also important to bear in mind that, as stated earlier, Piaget would not give the wide meaning to perception that some workers would. Thus any form of behaviour which involved the slightest degree of classification, inference or judgement would be judged by Piaget as an act of intelligence rather than of perception. This point is clearly brought out by the way in which he distinguishes the child's perception of space and the child's representation of space (103).

Piaget and Morf (104) describe a series of experiments which indicate that intellectual or quasi-intellectual processes may affect performance on perceptual tasks. One row of counters was placed parallel to another row (Figure 1) but in the one row the

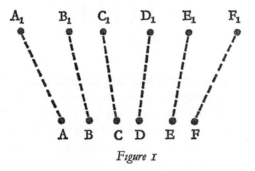

Figure 1

counters were spaced out more. The array was exposed for 1 second and the child had to judge if there were an equal number of counters in each row. Corresponding counters were also joined by bars AA_1, BB_1, etc. In another experiment the subject had to compare the length of two lines both with and without the use of reference circles (Figure 2). In a third task the child was faced with a number of rods parallel to, and equidistant from one another (Figure 3). He then had to judge if the difference in height between any one pair of adjacent rods was equal to that between another pair. If the imaginary line joining the top of the rods was a straight one then the subject could infer rather than merely see that the height difference between any two pairs of rods was the same.

Figure 2

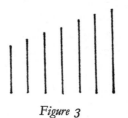

Figure 3

The upshot of the results was that at around 5 years of age children got little help from the supplementary information provided. Thus in the first experiment, the rods AA_1, BB_1, etc. made little difference to the perceptual judgements of the pupils. Then for a year or two a number of stages were found when such information was sometimes of help and sometimes not so that, for example, the connecting bars allowed the child to give a correct perceptual judgement when there were 4 counters, but less often when there were 6. By 8 years of age, however, the child could reason about the supplementary information provided and achieve a high degree of perceptual veridicality. From these kinds of experiments it seems that the young child relies on passive perceptions that centre on one feature of the situation and only later are his perceptions aided and abetted by more active processes such as intellectual operations.

Other experiments suggest that intellectual operations can also hinder veridical perception especially when new intellectual structures are just emerging. For example in one of Wursten's (140) experiments children were asked to judge which was the longer of two equal straight lines arranged as, say, in Figure 4.

|___

Figure 4

In such tasks there is an illusion with the length of the vertical over-estimated relative to the horizontal. The illusion was found to be very small at 5–6 years of age; it reached a maximum at 9–10 years and declined again after that age. In the case of adults the degree of illusion was about the same as an average 7- to 8-year-old. The explanation given for these findings suggested that at 5 to 6 years of age the child centred in turn on each line singly and did not bring the two together to form one configuration. Thus there was no distorting effect for one had no effect, as it were, on the other. Later on, the child commences to elaborate a system of rectilinear coordinates in Euclidean space, and once the two lines come to be regarded within a common spatial framework then the effect of one line on the other greatly increases the degree of the illusion. However from 9 or 10 years of age onwards the child can decrease the illusion somewhat by centring on each line again in turn although he is unable to reach the same degree of veridicality that he could before he was able to build a coordinate system. Other studies, too, have shown a curvelinear relationship between age and veridicality.

SOME CONCLUSIONS REGARDING PERCEPTION AND COGNITION

Simple forms of visual perception are present at birth, and by three months of age at the latest, past experience is modifying perception. Thereafter, perception increasingly directs action and behaviour and is itself modified by the child's increasing knowledge of objects and the environment generally. Later still it is affected by the growth of reasoning. The ability to discriminate becomes more accurate and the rapidity of perception increases due both to maturation and learning. Furthermore the older child attends to those aspects of the situation which give it meaning and significance for him, and which, thereby, help him to adapt, successfully, to the total situation.

The personality characteristics of children may also be of great importance in their perceptual development. For example, Witkin *et al.* (138) have shown that there are individual differences in children, from 8 upwards, in what they term 'field independence'. Thus field independent subjects as compared with field dependent subjects, can more easily find a diagram embedded in a larger more complex diagram and perform better on tasks involving spatial ability. Such individuals also seem to be more active, independent, self confident, they have more insight into and have less fear of their own impulses, are less tense and less prone to inferiority feelings, and seem more able to use the environment effectively for the satisfaction of their needs. Hence it is likely that personality structure can make it easier, or more difficult, for the individual to use his intelligence to understand the nature of the total situation, and because of this, personality seems likely to affect perceptual development.

INTERRELATIONS BETWEEN PERCEPTIONS DRAWN FROM MORE THAN ONE SENSE MODALITY

Few studies have been made of the interrelationships which might exist between auditory, haptic, kinaesthetic and visual perception. Such studies could be of consequence since perception arising through one sense might well be strengthened or weakened by perception arising through other sense modalities. Birch and Belmont (11) studied the growth of the ability to match a set of auditory stimuli – a set of taps – with a spatially distributed set of dots. The greatest improvement was shown between 5 and 7 years of age but improvement continued until 10. These workers also showed, as have Lovell and Gorton (81) that the ability to maintain this auditory-visual equivalence has only a small correlation with level of intelligence; also that poor readers make more errors than normal readers in equating auditory and visual patterns.

As we have already made clear, Piaget contends that perceptual development is an elaboration of sensori-motor activity. Piaget and Inhelder (103) studied the growth of haptic perception through tactile exploration. The subjects had to feel different shapes one by one without seeing them, and then identify each shape in turn by pointing to a drawing of it. They concluded that the first geometrical shapes that could be recognised via HAPTIC perception were those that involved closed versus open (e.g. an O from C) or intertwined figures. Such shapes were said to display topological relationships. The Geneva school explained this finding by claiming that in children aged 3 to 4 years tactile exploration is essentially global. Later there comes the ability to make a rough distinction between shapes with straight and curved sides, and then some further differentiation through angular properties. From 6 years of age onwards there is more methodical exploration of the shapes and children can distinguish between such complex euclidean shapes as stars and crosses. Lovell (75) replicated this study amongst children aged 2 years 11 months to 5 years 8 months and it was true that overall, children picked out shapes said to display topological relationships more easily than they could euclidean relationships. However, there was no evidence that shapes displaying topological relationships were more easily identified than euclidean shapes with curved edges. It seems that it is gaps, holes, points, corners etc. in euclidean space which make identification easier because the amount of information conveyed is greater. Likewise the writer's evidence supports the view of the Geneva school that the square, rhombus, rectangle and quadrilateral are the hardest to identify by haptic perception because the relatively straight sides convey little information. Again Fisher (37) has shown that when children have words that they can use to identify their tactile impressions, they can pick out euclidean shapes as easily if not more easily than those displaying topological relationships. Haptic perception certainly comes later than visual perception, but overall the views of the Geneva school on the growth of haptic perception have not been altogether confirmed by other workers.

D

PERCEPTION IN THE SCHOOL SITUATION

After having had some discussion of important theoretical issues we shall, in the remainder of this chapter, deal with some aspects of perception that are of immediate relevance to the teacher. Much important and very interesting material will have to be omitted. Readers interested in the development of perception of, say, colour space and movement should read the review by Rivoire and Kidd (106), while those interested in the growth of the perception of depth in children should consult the work of Walk and Gibson (131). Here there will be a short discussion of the question of perception and reading, and perception in relation to the interpretation of pictures and photographs.

Gibson *et al.* (44) have studied the growth of the ability to distinguish certain important features of forms which are much like letters. A number of standard letter-like forms were taken (Figure 5) and a series of transformations carried out on these. From the point of the child being able to

| Standard | Line to curve | 180° rotation | Close |

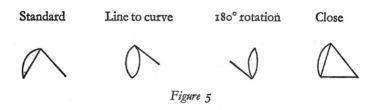

Figure 5

recognise ordinary letters of the alphabet three kinds of transformations were considered to be critical. These were the transformations of line to curve, rotation or reversal, and topological or open to closed. In reading, these transformations are found in the differences between V and U, between b and d or M and W, and between O and C respectively.

The task of the child was to examine the standard form and then to look along a row which contained one instance of the standard form along with all the transformations of that form. It was found that the number of errors of confusion involving both rotation and reversal transformations decreased from about 40 per cent at four years of age to 25 per cent at five, and to under 10 per cent at eight years of age. For the line to break transformation the percentage number of errors of confusion declined from 15 at four years of age to under 10 at eight years of age. The experiment was then repeated among 4- and 5-year-olds using twelve real letters as printed capitals using the same transformations. The medium correlation coefficient between confusion errors with the letter-like forms and with letters, for each of the transformations, was about + ·6. It would appear then that most children are able to discriminate between letters by between 5 and 6 years of age, with some children being able to do so much earlier. This is also the same general conclusion arrived at by Vernon (128) in reviewing earlier experimental studies. While the child undoubtedly learns much concerning the distinctive features of a set of letters on his own, the teacher also helps, as, for example, when she points out reversal errors, e.g. confusion between p and q. In one way or another, the significance of certain differentiating features of letters has to be learned. But we are not yet in a position to say if the child develops a schema for each specific letter, or whether he finds out in what ways each letter is unique and how it differs from others.

The growth of auditory perception has been discussed at length by Kidd and Kidd (64). There is a tendency towards greater auditory acuity and pitch discrimination with age, suggesting that maturation may be an important influence in the growth of auditory perception. However, it is difficult to say if maturation is affecting the young child's capacity to attend and his willingness to cooperate or whether it is affecting his perception *per se*. It seems likely that some children may be in trouble when the vowel sounds used in their environment are markedly different from those in standard English and hence, presumably, from those used by the teacher. This is particularly likely to be the case with monosyllabic words which are differentiated by only one vowel, e.g. 'mud' and 'mad'. It is true, of course, that many words will be recognised from their consonants but in the example quoted corrections of pronunciation of consonants will not help. One hopes that teachers will articulate all speech sounds accurately and clearly. At the same time they must recognise that a few children may have temporary problems in reading caused by auditory perception – not in the sense that perceptual development has been delayed or is faulty, but because in their everyday speech they have been used to faulty vowels and elided consonants, and in school they have to learn the sound patterns in the words which teacher speaks.

The interpretation of pictures and photographs is also a matter of consequence for the teacher. Hockberg and Brooks (55) studied a child whose vocabulary up to 19 months of age had been taught wholly by means of actual objects. While there were some pictures in his environment he was not given names or association for pictures. Yet when given pictures and line drawings of familiar objects at 19 months he recognised the pictures. In his case, at least, there was an irreducible minimum of natural ability for picture recognition and for response to certain formal features of lines on paper. Such recognition and response did not depend upon an association between picture and the object represented, or upon an association between a picture and a verbal response.

Hudson (56) studying groups from different cultural groups in Africa found that almost all subjects could identify pictures and line drawings of men and familiar animals. But many had difficulty in identifying perspective lines representing a road or lines giving a three dimensional 'look' to a hill. Even when a road or hill was identified it did not necessarily indicate that the subject had 'three dimensional perception'. Such perception did seem to depend to some extent upon both informal training and attendance at school. Schooling was not available to members of certain of the groups, but most interesting was the fact that cultural isolation retarded the growth of 3 D pictorial perception even in candidates possessing an advanced level of formal education. More recent work by Deregowski (25A) suggests that this relative impairment in 3D pictorial perception is due to the fact that in certain cultures children allocate lesser importance to depth cues than to other elements in the picture, and so restructure pictures differently than, say, European children. It seems likely that the mode of integration of the elements of a picture is a product of acculturation, for if depth cues are given enough prominence in the picture by the draughtsman, the same children do take account of them.

There is one report that lower class American children aged 3 to 5 years are less consistent in classifying pictures of objects (i.e. putting the pictures into categories or classes such as toys, things you write with) compared with the three dimensional life-sized objects, than are middle class children. The former children have more difficulty in classifying representational material even when there is no difference between the groups in identifying and labelling the pictures. This study does not bear upon the growth of perception *per se* but it does show that there are class differences in the relationship between intelligence and perception.

Although the ability to identify objects in pictures comes by 2 to 3 years of age and may be universal, teachers must be on their guard against expecting too much by way of picture interpretation. By the time the average child leaves the infant school at 7 + years he can talk about the activities which simple pictures show people to be doing. But it is not until the end of the junior school or the beginning of the secondary school period that average pupils can understand the meaning a picture suggests of events not actually shown. Thus one of the pictures in the 1937 Terman–Merrill revision of the Binet Intelligence Test for 12-year-olds shows the picture of a telegraph boy waving to a car to stop and give him a lift. By the side is a bicycle with a wheel which has come off. Average pupils do not give the meaning of the picture until 12 years of age. It is important, too, for the teacher to realise that young children are as likely to pay attention to quite irrelevant details in a picture as they are to those items which are vital for comprehending the point of the picture. They are also likely to notice, particularly, those things which are familiar or understandable to them. Thus pictures in geography, history or literature showing people in strange costumes or in situations which are not recognised by them, may be quite outside their understanding without help from the teacher and further reading.

FURTHER READING

Birch, H. G. and Lefford, A. 'Visual Differentiation, Intersensory Integration, and Voluntary Motor Control', *Monogr. Soc. Res. Child Developm.*, 32 (2) (1967)

Gibson, E. J. in *Child Psychology*, chapter 4 (Chicago, National Society for the Study in Education 1963)

Kidd, A. H. and Rivoire, J. L. (Eds.), *Perceptual Development in Children*, chapters 6 and 14 (University of London Press 1967)

Munn, N. L. *The Evolution and Growth of Human Behaviour*, chapter 9 (Boston, Houghton Mifflin 1955)

Piaget, J. *et al*. in *The Developmental Psychology of Jean Piaget*, by Flavell, J. H., pp. 31–3, 225–36 (London, Van Nostrand 1963)

Schaffer, H. R. and Parry, M. H. 'Perceptual-Motor Behaviour in Infancy as a Function of Age and Stimulus Familiarity', *Brit. J. Psychol.*, 60, 1–9 (1969)

Vernon, M. D. *The Psychology of Perception*, chapters 2 and 6 (London, University of London Press 1962)

Vernon, M. D. 'Perception and Perceptual Learning', *Development in Learning* 2 (Eds. Lunzer, E. A. and Morris, J. F.) (London, Staples 1968)

4 The Acquisition of Language

Children usually begin to talk somewhere between the 18th and 21st months of life and by about the fourth birthday have learnt much of the fundamental structure of their language. Why is this so? One current view, powerfully argued by Lenneberg (72) is that the onset of language is controlled by a maturational process. From a study of both normal and abnormal children he also concludes that the language maturational process must be independent of motor-skeletal and other forms of maturation. Once some minimum level of intellectual growth has been reached, the onset of language is not dependent on intelligence *per se* for there are children who are of normal intelligence, have no neurological and psychiatric symptoms, and yet are delayed in producing two- and three-word-sentences. Again, Lenneberg maintains that the influence of a very great variety of environmental conditions leaves unchanged the age of onset of language although the development of language may be markedly affected. McNeill (86) on the other hand, while subscribing to the view that the capacity for language is innate, seems to think that language acquisition depends on some more general mechanism which underpins many different kinds of cognitive problem.

There are, however, others who while not denying the view that language acquisition must have some constitutional basis specific to the human species, think that it is too early to be dogmatic about the nature of the innate mechanisms. For example, Donaldson (28) asks whether the great development that goes on during the sensori-motor stage of intelligence might possibly serve in some degree as a preparation for speech that emerges between eighteen and twenty-four months of age. However, nothing further will be said about the nature of the innate basis of language as no doubt it will continue to be discussed for a long time to come. Our topic of language acquisition will be treated first from the earlier point of view of what may be called normative studies, and then from the viewpoint of developmental psycholinguistics.

THE FIRST YEAR

We are greatly indebted to workers such as Bagley, Shirley, C. Buhler, Gesell and Thomson, etc. for many of the earlier studies of the growth of language. It is true that these investigators were not trained in phonetics, nor did they employ modern recording aids, but they did provide a very great deal of basic information. Much of their data has been reported by McCarthy (85).

In the first two months of life vocalisations are clearly recognisable as in such utterances as *ah, eh, uh*, and at the same time the infant makes differentiated cries for discomfort and pain. During the following two months the baby will begin to turn his head in the direction of a speaking human voice, while between the third and sixth month vocalisations indicating pleasure, displeasure and other states of feeling are in evidence. From the sixth month onwards the infant appears to begin to imitate sounds in a very rudimentary way and say, for example, *ma*, whereas by eight months of age he can indicate recognition of an object by a vocalisation and produce a two-syllable-utterance where the second is a repetition of the first, e.g. *ma ma*. Between the eighth and twelfth months new skills emerge; the child listens to familiar words, understands gestures, can wave 'goodbye' and often say one word. Thereafter steady progress is maintained for by about the fifteenth month the infant can carry out simple commands, e.g. 'give me' and his vocabulary increases.

There has been much discussion regarding the role of imitation by the child in the acquisition of speech sound. Lewis (73) for example, summarising the literature at that time indicated that there seemed to be three broad views held in respect of the phenomenon of imitation: that there is an innate tendency for the child to respond to speech by speech; that the child responds by expression to expression; that vocal responses to speech arise from intervention of the adult into the child's activity of babbling. However, Lewis himself contended in respect of the third view that hearing an adult word merely stimulates the child to utter his own babbling sounds and because of this the child may become trained to respond with a particular sound to a particular heard sound. The position is now thought to be complicated for Lenneberg (71) has some evidence that during the first year of life infant vocalisation is acoustically different from the corresponding sounds made by 3-year-olds and adults. For example, Lenneberg showed that when the cooing of a 3-month-old infant was compared using a spectrogram (this shows the variation of the frequency of the sound – in cycles per second – with time) with the sounds made by the mother in imitating the cooing, clear differences were in evidence. Again Lenneberg (71) has shown that neither deafness nor deaf parents reduces the amount of sound activity in the first six months of life to any extent. The speech sounds of deaf and hearing children are, qualitatively, almost identical in the first three months of life while even between the fourth and twelfth months many of the sounds uttered by the deaf are much like those of hearing infants. But after the latter age the sounds of deaf and hearing children increasingly differ. These findings throw doubt upon the role of imitation, and question whether the child's first motivation for speech development lies in the discovery of the similarity of the sounds made by himself and his mother.

It seems clear that gesture is understood by the child before he understands words, just as he uses gestures before he uses language. For example, he stretches his arms out for objects long before he can ask for them. Lewis (73) points out that response to gestures does not appear to take place before response to intonational patterns of speech, i.e. he distinguishes, say, between friendly and angry talk. Indeed, Lewis concludes from the literature that responses to differences in intonation may even come slightly before response to gesture, or, at least, each may facilitate the effect of the other.

Although it is difficult to say what a child's first word is, there is agreement that it consists of the repetition of a monosyllable such as *ma ma* or *bye bye*. Lewis, Irwin, and other workers, agree that the early words consist of single or duplicated syllables in which the consonants are made with both lips, or with lip against teeth or tongue against teeth, e.g. b, v, n. The first words are used on their own and are usually nouns or interjections. But they are not used in the same sense as they are later. The word *mummy* may not just refer to a person, but may indicate that something needs to be done for the child, in much the same way as when we adults shout *fire* it indicates a fire in progress and that something needs doing about it. By using gesture and intonation together he can also convey a number of meanings with one word. The early words are strongly affective and they indicate feelings, needs and wishes. It will be, of course, appreciated that there is a psychological gap between the utterance of the phonetic form of a word and its correct representational use. As Sapir (108) pointed out – the phonetic framework of speech does not constitute the inner fact of language.

THE GROWTH OF VOCABULARY

Many workers such as Ammons *et al.* (3), Smith, M. E. (116) and Smith, M. K. (117) in the USA, also Burns (19) and Watts (134) in Great Britain, have studied the growth of vocabulary in children. Note carefully that there is a difference between the number of words one can use or one's active vocabulary, and the number of words one can understand or one's passive vocabulary. The latter is much larger than the former. Generalising from a number of these studies, it is clear that the average number of words in the active vocabulary of ordinary children increases as follows: 3 words at twelve months, 20 words at eighteen months, 300 words at twenty-four months, 900 to 1000 words at thirty-six months and at least 2000 words when the child enters school at five years of age. These figures will, of course, be much less in children of low intelligence and in those coming from seriously deprived circumstances. At the same time there is considerable development in the child's language structure, so that while the average child is forming his first two-word phrase at around twenty months of age, before his fourth birthday he is using well formed sentences and complex grammatical rules. This point will be developed later in the chapter.

The size of the active vocabulary goes on increasing after five years of age. By the time the child enters junior school it is at least 4000 words according to Watts (134). Thereafter the number of words used increases less quickly. Terman suggested a vocabulary of 5,400, 7,200, and 9,000 words for average American children aged 10, 12 and 14 years of age respectively. However, there is a rapid increase in the size of the child's passive vocabulary from around the time he enters school and begins to read. Thus Smith (117) showed that the average number of words recognised (in terms of Smith's definition) by American children increases from about 17,000 at seven years of age, to over 30,000 at eleven to twelve years of age. It is important for the teacher to understand that the child can get the meaning, both from hearing and seeing in print, of words that he cannot use.

SOME BASIC NOTIONS IN CURRENT PSYCHOLINGUISTICS

In the writer's judgement linguists sometimes use terms which are not clearly defined. This makes the understanding of their work by teachers more difficult than it need otherwise be. Bearing this in mind let us consider some of the basic notions in current psycholinguistics. Chomsky (23), like some other linguists and psychologists, makes a basic distinction between linguistic competence and linguistic performance. The former term indicates a native speaker's knowledge of, and intuitions about, his language, while performance is the expression of competence in talking. Because a child's linguistic performance is poor, it does not necessarily mean that his competence is also. A major task for psycholinguistics is to establish the nature of the mechanisms that underlie competence as Sutherland (121) has pointed out.

Another important distinction made by Chomsky (23) is that sentences must be characterised by two structural descriptions; by their surface structures and by their base or underlying structures. The need for two such descriptions can be seen by considering the case of the imperative. 'Come here' is a surface structure. It is well understood by ordinary speakers as a realisation of the base structure, 'You will come here'. Evidence for such a statement lies in the fact that the words can be reordered to ask a

question of the form, 'Come here, will you?'. This is grammatical, whereas there are no sentences like 'Come here, did he?'.
It will be noted that the meaning was given to the base structure,
and the transformation to a surface structure did not change its
meaning.

At the present time grammar is divided into morphology and
syntax, and in the view of Chomsky and his followers the syntactic component is a description of the nature of the relations
(this is deep structure) that link up the parts of the sentence and
hence influence the meaning of the sentence. Furthermore, the
syntactic component is also the phrasing (this is surface structure)
of the linear string of words which are the basis for the output of
the phonetic component. Thus the deep structure of the sentence
embodies the essential features of relations and meaning, and
these may be transformed (by deletions, substitutions and per-
mutations of words) into a surface structure and then into sound.
When a listener recognises speech he has, of course, to extract
the deep structure of the utterance from the surface structure.

EARLY GRAMMARS

Before we indicate some examples of early child grammars it is
well to bear in mind a warning given by Chomsky. He has pointed
out that before we discover anything really fundamental about
child grammars, it will be necessary to use many and varied
means of observing the child's performance and comprehension
in very differing kinds of circumstances. Only then shall we be
able to determine his linguistic competence at any stage in his
development. Direct description of the child's actual output is
unlikely to do this. Bearing this clear warning in mind we pro-
ceed to consider some of the experimental studies which have
thrown some light on the regularities of children's language
although the performance was obtained in very limited areas of the
child's daily life and action.

By the second birthday, or just before, children begin to use
two and three word sentences. These are much abbreviated
compared with those that adults use and consist of utterances
such as 'all gone milk', 'two shoe', 'Mary make tea' and 'cake

here'. This had been termed 'telegraphic' speech. The child tends to omit certain classes of words such as articles and prepositions, leaves out inflections (-s from shoes and -ing from making) or puts together words which form an ungrammatical (judged by adult speech) combination. Nevertheless the child seems to possess a simple grammar.

These early grammars have been studied by Miller and Ervin (91), Braine (13), Brown and Bellugi (15) and others. One very common arrangement is the putting together of words from what Braine calls the 'pivot' and 'open' classes. Examples of the former are 'all gone', 'see', 'my'; and of the latter 'leg', 'hat', 'daddy'. Words in the pivot class are relatively fewer than those in the open class and they tend to resemble function words rather than content words although the pivot class does contain certain adjectives. But the early sentences also contain the juxtaposition of two words from the open class such as 'hat daddy'. It seems as if some of the elementary competence of children at this age might be represented by Sentence→(Pivot Class) + Open class or

$$S \rightarrow (P) + O \qquad \text{(Rule 1)}$$

The P is in brackets because the open, but not the pivot class words can stand on their own.

A great deal of what we know about the early grammars of children comes from the Language Acquisition Project at Harvard. Thus Brown and Bellugi (15) have indicated how the pivot class becomes differentiated. Although they studied talkative children of educated middle class parents, their suggestions indicate the general direction of development in all children as far as is known. When they first tested the child (time, t_1) his utterance was of the form P + N (noun). The pivot class words in Brown and Bellugi's example consisted of the words 'a', 'my', 'that', 'two', so we might encounter, at that stage, a sentence such as 'that doll'. Some 4 months later (time, t_2) they found the pivot class has become differentiated into a demonstrative pronoun, an article, a new pivot class word and a noun.

Thus at time t_2

$$S \rightarrow (\text{Dem.}) + (\text{Art.}) + (P) + N \qquad \text{(Rule 2)}$$

At this stage we may find the child saying 'that a my doll', or 'that a car' when the pivot class word is omitted. It can be seen that by this time the child has come to treat demonstrative pronouns and articles as unique classes and the pivot class is reduced in membership.

After a further 2 months (time t_3) Brown and Bellugi found a further subdivision of the pivot class, for the child appeared to have made separate classes for adjectives and possessive pronouns. Thus the pivot class word had been replaced to give:

$$S \rightarrow (Art.) + (Adj.) + N \qquad (Rule\ 3)$$

This would give a sentence of the type, 'a yellow doll'. Alternately we might find:

$$(P)/(Dem.)/(Poss.) + N \qquad (Rule\ 4)$$

yielding sentences such as 'other cup', 'this doll', 'your car'. There is also a further possible subdivision of the pivot class word giving adjectives the unique privilege of appearing after nouns:

$$S \rightarrow (Art.) + N + (Adj.) \qquad (Rule\ 5)$$

This leads to a sentence such as 'a doll big'. So within the space of 6 months, five grammatical classes merged, namely, articles, adjectives, demonstrative pronouns, possessive pronouns and a residual pivot class.

The story is now taken up by McNeill (86) who points out that the pivot / open class construction is not the only one present in children's early grammars for they also form sentences of the open / open type some of which are covered by the rule:

$$S \rightarrow N + N \qquad (Rule\ 6)$$

Typical utterances in this case would be 'Mary doll', 'daddy hat'.

However, sentences illustrated by rules 1 to 6 do not possess say hierarchical structure (i.e. natural breaks into their constituents) yet sentences with such structure are found in early grammars. One such type of sentence can be illustrated by:

$$S \rightarrow (P) + NP \text{ (noun phrase)} \qquad (Rule\ 7)$$
$$NP \rightarrow \begin{Bmatrix} (P) + N \\ N + N \end{Bmatrix}$$

Whereas under Rule 1 the child would say 'that shoe', and under

Rule 6 'John shoe', Rule 7 would permit 'that my shoe' or 'that John shoe'.

Another kind of sentence which was found can be illustrated as follows:

$$S \rightarrow \text{predicate phrase} \quad \text{(Rule 8)}$$
$$\text{predicate phrase} - \text{Verb} + \text{NP}$$
$$\text{NP} \rightarrow \left\{ \begin{array}{c} \text{(P)} + \text{N} \\ \text{N} + \text{N} \end{array} \right\}$$

An example of this rule would be 'want that shoe' or 'want John shoe'.

At time t_1, most sentences comprised the Rules 1, 6 and 8 although the choice of P in Rule 8 was not often taken. So the majority of sentences consisted of a pivot word followed by a noun ('that doll'), or noun plus noun ('Mary hat'), or verb plus noun ('want doll'), and sometimes noun plus verb 'John go'. Again the majority of the three word sentences at time t_1 followed Rule 8 and used the noun + noun alternative of NP, so that a typical sentence would be 'drink John milk'. When observations were made at time t_2 no new patterns appeared in the child's grammar, but Rule 7 was more frequently in evidence and three word sentences were found. Likewise at time t_3 there were no new rules but a greater frequency of sentences formed by Rules 7 and 8.

As we have seen, Rule 7 produces the noun phrase and Rule 8 the predicate phrase of adult grammar. So these early grammars generate the major constituents of well formed sentences, although at that age it is only rarely that they are juxtaposed to make such sentences. But later the noun phrase and the predicate phrase will be put together to form the major constituents of well-formed adult sentences. We shall then have:

$$S \rightarrow N + V + N \quad \text{(Rule 7 plus Rule 8)}$$

yielding a sentence such as 'Boy wants shoe' or 'I caught horse'. Equally we could have:

$$S \rightarrow N + N + V \quad \text{('John car goes')}$$

or

$$S \rightarrow N + V \quad \text{'Mary eat'}$$

So we find that the young child's early grammatical competence includes basic grammatical classes, basic grammatical rules and basic grammatical relations (i.e. 'subject of the sentence', 'predicate of the sentence', and 'object of the verb'). Moreover these are all properties of the base structure of a sentence. Thus in their early speech we do not find children using transformational rules; that is, the child does not yet through transformation delete, substitute or permute elements in a way that the phrase structure rules described above cannot. A little later such transformations will commence. For example, Brown, Cazden and Bellugi (16) show that some of the earliest transformational rules in the children they are studying perform such grammatical functions as: agreement in person and number for subject and verb, creation of such possessives as *yours*, and the deletion of the subject from imperatives (e.g. 'come here' not 'you come here'). So from around 3 years of age onwards the child increasingly uses grammars like those of adults. Indeed, Menyuk (89A, 89B) using Chomsky's generative framework, has listed the transformational rules used to generate the sentences obtained from a sample of nursery, kindergarten and 6-year-old children.

McNeill (86) in a most stimulating paper has discussed the problem of accounting for noun and predicate phrases in children's speech, that is, by what mechanism they discover these natural breaks or major constituents, i.e. hierarchical structures. He argues against the imitation of adult speech, the appeal to 'creative abilities', or the value of the distribution or frequency of occurrence of noun and predicate phrases in parental speech since they give the child no more than examples to imitate. The essential feature of hierarchical structures is that they are hierarchical, yet this is abstract and not marked in speech. Nevertheless children do discover these structures and this suggests to many that there is a case of positing an innate linguistic capacity or some kind of faculty of language since almost all children's early sentences seem to be produced by rules 7 and 8. Moreover, it is difficult to explain basic grammatical relations, unless they too are part of some innate linguistic capacity, for the child certainly does seem to express the relations he intends to express right from the start. This being so, basic grammatical relations should be universal.

Indeed, Greenberg's (46) study suggests that this is in fact the case, for in a survey of thirty languages he found none that was lacking such concepts. Thus a child who had such concepts could begin to learn any language by finding out how each of the grammatical rules was expressed locally. So perhaps subject and object relations are to the child what some instinctive piece of behaviour is to the animal – there is an innate pattern awaiting a releaser to set it in operation.

Klima and Bellugi (65) have made some suggestions for stages in respect of the use of negatives and questions. In the case of the former they propose:

Stage 1

Here there is a prefixing of the words 'no' or 'not' to the structure of Rule 8 as in 'no hurt hand', 'not . . . bad', 'milk no'.

Stage 2

Some 3 to 6 months later there is a growth in the number of negative forms in evidence but still little sign of transformations. Negatives appear in imperatives ('don't go'); in connection with Rules 7 and 8 ('I no want tea'); and the words 'don't' and 'can't' appear as separate vocabulary ('I don't hear you') in connection with certain verbs. Of course, a sentence such as 'I don't hear you' is found in adult grammar. However, it is not thought that the child is transforming at this stage because auxiliary verbs do not yet occur in questions or declarative utterances (e.g. 'I do hear you'). The child can also understand the negative embedded in the auxiliary of the sentence. For example:

Mother: I can't wash you right now.
Child: Why not?

Stage 3

In another 3 to 6 months there is a further progression and we find sentences such as 'John didn't cry', 'This not milk', 'I don't hear it'. But auxiliary verbs also occur in the child's questions and declarative utterances (e.g. 'I can see you') so there are grounds for believing that the -nt is a negative element in its own right separate from the auxiliary verb. The child is beginning to use transformations.

E

Readers interested in the stages in the growth of children's questions should read the tentative suggestions put forward by Klima and Bellugi. Brown has indicated that until the mean length of the utterance reaches about 2·8 MORPHEMES children's questions are of a very simple type, e.g. 'what dat?'. Such questions are either routine utterances for certain situations or they are of a non-transformational type. When the mean length of the utterance equals or exceeds 2·8 then we find an increasing variety of related wh questions 'who, whom, what, where, when, why and how' involving transformations. One sort of wh question, the *why* question, seems to be derived from a direct transform of an antecedent declaration by the mother. For example, a declarative sentence of the type 'He was throwing the ball' or 'I think the baby is asleep' leads to such questions as 'why he throwing the ball?' and 'why is baby asleep?'

It seems that by about 4 years of age English speaking children have learned much of the fundamental structure of their language – long before the onset of the stage of concrete operational thought. There have been few structural analyses of language after 5 years of age, but in general it seems that from 4 to 5 years of age onwards there is a period of overlearning as it were so that grammar becomes automatic. But some linguistic structures are not available in certain situations until the onset of concrete operational thought as we shall see later. The less frequently used linguistic patterns such as the use of the word *too* with positive sentences, and *either* with negative sentences still have to be learned. There have, of course, been studies of the growth of sentence length with age. McCarthy (85) summarises much of the earlier literature and suggests that by 6½ years of age the mean length of sentence is about 5 words, while by 8 years of age it has levelled off at 7 to 8 words. However, we shall see below that more recent work indicates that the mean sentence length has now increased.

One important study is that of Templin (125). She analysed twenty-four thousand utterances of children aged 3 to 8 years of age, from the point of view of length, grammatical complexity, grammatical accuracy and parts of speech used. The same pattern of growth in respect of sentence length and complexity, and in the use of various parts of speech, were found as in earlier studies.

But compared with 25 years earlier, responses were found to be longer and children used more complex sentences and adverb clauses. It is possible that greater parent-child dialogue, mass media, and better schooling all contributed to this. Templin also found:

1. A considerable increase with age of the use of subordinate clauses. This was true in respect of all the socio-economic groups and for both sexes. In general there was an increase with age in the use of more complex and elaborate forms of sentence.

2. A decrease with age in the proportion of structurally incomplete but functionally complete remarks. Such remarks include: expletives; naming; answers in which words are implied because they are expressed in the question; and remarks which are not complete in themselves but which are clearly a continuation of the preceding remark.

3. Significant differences in length of utterance as between boys and girls were only rarely found. But children from the upper socio-economic groups tended to use slightly longer utterances at most of the age levels although at only two age levels were the differences statistically significant. Again children from the higher socio-economic groups tended to use a more advanced type of sentence structure but the differences were not very great. However, it should be noted that in the area in which Templin carried out her study there are not as great cultural differences generally between the socio-economic groups as there are in some American urban areas.

A study carried out under the author's direction (Lovell, 82) investigated the speech of children whose speech was retarded but who were otherwise normal. The ages of the children ranged from 3 years 4 months to 4 years 7 months and the total number of utterances made by individual subjects ranged from 7 to 37 when each was observed during four hours of play. The mean number of morphemes per utterance for each child varied from 1·6 to 2·8. It was found that almost all the utterances could be described in terms of the eight rules of phrase structure grammar already described. The negatives found were of the type used in stages 1 and 2.

The results showed clearly that not only is the amount of speech of these children seriously below normal, but their linguistic structures are seriously deficient judged against normal speakers of the same chronological age. But it does seem that the suggested rules and stages are applicable not only to speaking American children but also to speech retarded British pupils.

A POSSIBLE EXPLANATION FOR LANGUAGE CHANGE

McNeill (86) has proposed a plausible explanation for the changes seen in child language. The first words used have been termed 'holophrasic' for they have more meanings for a child than they have for adults. For example, the word 'teddy' may mean 'I want teddy', 'Teddy on floor', 'Teddy not here'. But if his speech consisted of a dictionary of holophrasic words it would entail a heavy load for the child's memory, and such a dictionary would be susceptible to ambiguity. This might lead to the creation of a dictionary of sentences. But this, too, is abandoned by the child for the memory load would again be very great, there would again be the problem of ambiguity, and the meaning of a sentence could only be made clear by knowing its context. But by changing over to a dictionary of words supplemented by rules of syntax and semantics, the child reduces the number of interpretations which he has to remember. Moreover, he can thereby increase the variety of his sentences and so attain greater precision of expression by being able to say exactly what he wants to say.

GROWTH OF MORPHOLOGY

In English speaking children there is consistent word ordering before inflexion, whereas in more heavily inflected language, syntax and morphology grow up more alongside one another. Berko (9) was the first to test the growth of English morphology in children. A technique was developed in which children were asked to make new formations using nonsense words. For example a child was shown a picture of an object and told, 'This is a lun'. Another picture was then shown of two such objects and the experimenter continued, 'Now there are two of them. These are two . . .'. The correct answer is, of course, 'luns'. The ages of the subjects ranged from 4 to 7 years of age. Generalising from the results it can be said that most of the children could in uncomplicated cases, form a plural by adding -*s* by 6 to 7 years of age. But at the same age only about a third of the subjects could add -*es* to form *tasses* or *kazhes* in spite of the fact that almost all could manage *glasses*. In respect of the past tense most of the older children could add an -*ed* to form *glinged*, or *ricked*, but only about a third could produce *motted* and *bodded* and even less could formulate *rang*. All the subjects found compounding and the derivation of new words difficult. For example, there were few satisfactory replies when subjects were asked what they would call a man who *zibbed* for a living, what name they would give a very tiny *wug*, what they would call a house a *wug* lives in, and what kind of a dog a dog covered with *quirks* is. Again, Berko's subjects gave few satisfactory answers when asked to analyse compound words such as *blackboard*.

Miller and Ervin (91) used some of the techniques with younger children and established that the plural was known by three years of age although there were great individual differences. The plurals for lexicon words were always known before those of nonsense words with a similar shape, but the time lag was small.

From the studies mentioned above together with that of Lovell and Bradbury (78) into the growth of morphology among Educationally Subnormal Special School pupils, it looks as if the rules involving many of the inflections in English can be elaborated by the flexible schemas of the preoperational stage of thought. But some of the more difficult inflections remain a stumbling block for the six-year-old who will still use *brang* and *brought* or *bought* and *buyed* interchangeably. However, compounding and the derivation of new words, together with the analysis of compound words, does necessitate an ability on the part of the child to monitor his own thinking, that is, he needs to have reached the stage of concrete operational thought.

THE ROLE OF ADULT SPEECH

There are certain similarities in the grammars of natural languages which are attributable to the general form of language *per se*. In so far as these similarities can be shown to hold for languages everywhere they are described as language universals. According to McNeill (86) adult speech aids the child in choosing between a narrow set of possibilities defined by language universals. While a child is committed to a noun phrase and predicate phrase format for sentences it is adult speech which enables the child to determine in which order they appear.

Practice in the sense of repeating adult grammar may play a part in the acquisition of language, but its value is not clear at present. Nor do we know the importance of language expansion. When the child says 'Daddy tea', the adult may expand this into 'Daddy has had his tea', 'Dad eats his tea', 'Daddy will have his tea'. Each of the expanded sentences involves the same rules as those involved in generating the child's sentence. But it is the adult who must judge, from considerations other than linguistic ones, which of the expansions is the correct one in the situation, and it may well be that it is this expansion of child sentences by adults which provides models to show the child those parts of linguistic competence not completely determined by language universals. On the other hand it may be it is the mere provision of good models of adult speech and not the expansion of child language *per se* that is most valuable.

It is thus likely that when children are subjected to good models in one way or another they are likely to acquire language more quickly. Whenever parents take an interest in what their children have to say, and generally tend to subscribe to middle class rearing practices regardless of their own social class, they are likely to aid their children's acquisition of language. This point of view is generally in line with the viewpoint of Bernstein (10) while children who are not so privileged are forced to find out for themselves the appropriate English manifestation of the linguistic universals. Note carefully, however, that these children may not necessarily be lacking in linguistic competence. Finally, we may note that Cazden's (22A) study suggests that within middle class homes – not homes where there is a marked restriction in the use of language – variations in the child's linguistic environment as reflected in the parent-child interaction, may not greatly affect the learning of basic grammatical structures but rather how the child uses language to express ideas.

THE IMITATION, COMPREHENSION AND PRODUCTION OF SPEECH

Fraser, Bellugi and Brown (39) compared the performance of children in respect of the tasks of imitation (I), comprehension (C) and production (P) of speech using ten grammatical contrasts: viz., mass noun / count noun; singular / plural, marked by inflections; singular / plural, marked by 'is' and 'are'; present progressive tense / past tense; present progressive tense / future tense; affirmative / negative; singular / plural, of 3rd person possessive pronouns; subject / object, in the active voice; subject / object, in the passive voice; indirect object / direct object. They examined twelve 3-year-old American children and found that imitation was more advanced than comprehension and comprehension more advanced than production. Lovell and Dixon (80) have repeated this study, with some changes in procedures, with one hundred British children between 2 and 6 years of age, and with eighty children in ESN Special Schools. It was found that at all age levels, and in both categories of children, was imitation more advanced than comprehension, and comprehension to be more advanced than production. Furthermore, the rank difficulty of the items remained remarkably constant across tasks, across age levels for items within a given task, for items within a given task across normal and ESN Special School pupils, and for items within a given task across British and American 3-year-olds.

In the study of speech retarded children referred to earlier it was shown that on the ICP test they scored as high on C as did members of a control group of children who were speaking normally. They were, of course, seriously behind the members of the control group in respect of I and P scores. In other words for the speech retarded group we found C>I>P. When the speech of these pupils improves we shall no doubt find I>C>P as in the case of the educationally subnormal special school pupils and normal pupils.

McNeill (86) proposes that there may be at least three memory spans of different capacities involved in linguistic performance. The largest appears to be that for phonological production, the smallest that for grammatical production, and one of intermediate size for grammatical comprehension. Whether or not the child performs correctly on a given item, i.e. in his performance he preserves the given grammatical contrast, will depend on the length of the sentence he is required to operate relative to the size of the appropriate memory span.

Again since the child does appear to benefit from well formed sentences produced by adults, through expansion of his own sentences or by other means, it could be that a child's additions to his linguistic competence arise through his comprehension.

THE RELATIONSHIP BETWEEN LANGUAGE AND THOUGHT

The relationship between language and thought is a complex one. On this problem the Geneva school disagrees with the Harvard School of Cognitive Studies, while the Russian point of view is even further removed from that of Geneva.

One of the clearest statements of the Geneva school on this topic is found in Inhelder and Piaget's study of the growth of classification and seriation. They point out that all nouns and adjectives divide reality into classes, so that when children begin to use language a beginning of classification must be imposed by language. On the other hand, seriations are seldom elaborated completely in any language as, for example, in the series 'grandfather' through to 'grandson', although seriations are sometimes suggested by certain grammatical forms such as the comparative and superlative. So at the outset they envisaged the following alternatives: (1) the formation of classification and seriation is attributable solely to the use of language; (2) language could act as an accelerator in this respect; (3) language is necessary for the completion of the mental structures underlying these two processes but is insufficient to explain the formation of such structures. Inhelder and Piaget then carried out an analysis of the work which had been done with the deaf to that date and made a careful study of their own data bearing on the growth of preconcepts and concepts. They concluded that language contributes to the formation and stabilisation of a system of communication made possible by concepts, but is insufficient to explain the formation of the mental operations which permit the building of concepts, and which are the very essence of logical thought. They would not deny that language is a contributory factor in the growth of operational thought, but they would deny that operations arise directly out of language or that language is central to their development. For them, language acts largely as a symbolic vehicle for thought.

In a further study by Inhelder, Bovet, Sinclair and Smock (59) an examination was made of the spontaneous descriptions of children in various conservation tasks. It was found that there were differences in the linguistic structures used by those who conserved and those who did not. Inhelder and her colleagues concluded that language training, like any other form of training, helps to direct the child's interactions with the environment and so tends to focus the child's attention to relevant dimensions in the task situation. On the other hand there was no evidence that language training *per se* contributes to the build up of operational thought which is necessary for the achievement of conservation. These workers argue that language does not provide a kind of 'lens' which affects the way in which the child sees the world; rather the organisation of the perceptual world is brought about by the increasing interiorisation of actions to form operations, that is, by the growth of intelligence. At the same time they concede that there may well be a feedback of language on operational structures particularly at the level of formal thought when reasoning may be more closely tied to language. In summary then it may be said that for the Geneva school, language helps in the selection, storage and retrieval of information, but not in the coordination of input information; such coordination is linked more with intellectual growth.

It must be emphasised that the position might be different at the level of formal thought in which the subject formulates and tests hypotheses based on all possible combinations of variables. He then formulates laws relating to general categories of variables that are divorced from the concrete empirical data at hand. It is possible that language retardation denies the pupil the terms which aid the direct manipulation and understanding of relationships between abstractions thus resulting in a slower transition from concrete to formal operational thought. However, it is not known for certain if this is indeed the case.

In connection with the general problem of the relationship between thought and language the work of Furth (42) is relevant. He has produced much evidence which suggests that the performance of deaf children with severe linguistic restriction is often not much different from that of hearing children on tests that use non-verbal manifestations of intelligent behaviour. In his view, up to 12 or 13 years of age the basic ability to conceptualise and reason is largely independent of language and mainly subject to the experience of living. For Furth it is mainly the paucity of experience which is so detrimental to deaf children, not lack of language.

The views of J. S. Bruner (17) of Harvard are somewhat different. He points out that by around 4 years of age much of the fundamental structure of the mother tongue has been acquired, certainly long before the onset of concrete operational thought. For some years thereafter the child can muster words and form sentences but he cannot, in corresponding fashion, organise the things of the real world or his experience, which the words and sentences stand for. For some years there is a partial divorce between syntax and semantics so that the meanings of words often remain imprecise and childish, and the implications of what is said are not thoroughly grasped. Thus children and adults can often talk without much thought being involved at all.

Bruner points out that in a typical conservation experiment a 5-year-old may well say that one quantity is less than the other, the next moment that it is more, and then that they are the same. In Bruner's view it is not until the child inspects his language, that he goes back over his experience to check for match or mis-match between what he says and what he sees. He must, essentially, treat the utterance as a sentence and recognise any contradiction at that level. Then the child can go back to his experience and see the world differently because of the language that reorders his experience. It is not, of course, language in itself which provides the reordering of experience, but the recognition of contradiction at the level of language that enables the child to go back to reality and restructure the experience. Hence for Bruner thought comes to conform to language. While some minimum level of mental growth is necessary before language is possible at all, once the latter is in use it refines thought, and it is possible by using language as an instrument to scale to higher levels of thought.

The Russians believe that speech plays a very important role indeed in the growth of thought. Vygotsky (130) claims that thought and speech have different roots and that they develop along different lines and are independent of one another. Nevertheless lack of language must inhibit higher levels of thought although he stressed that there is no clear cut or constant correlation between language and thought – their relationship undergoes many changes. Vygotsky looked again at Piaget's (98) notions of EGOCENTRIC and SOCIALISED SPEECH found in pre-school children. In the former there is no attempt on the part of the child to adapt his speech to the needs of the listener or even to make sure he is listening. Basically there is no real attempt to communicate. In socialised speech, however, there is the clear intention to communicate and to make or persuade the listener to adopt some course of action. For Piaget, egocentric speech disappeared as the child approached 7 years of age as it no longer had any useful role to play in his behaviour. Vygotsky disagreed, and argued that egocentric speech went underground and became 'inner speech'. Furthermore, this internalised speech, in which the child can think words instead of pronouncing them, can serve both autistic ends and the growth of logical thought. Other distinguished Russian workers in this general field such as Luria (84) and Galperin (43) hold that speech is a major factor in the growth of mental structures and concept formation. For example Luria writes (Luria 84) 'Language is not only a means of generalisation, it is at the same time the source of thought'.

It can be seen at once that there is a considerable degree of disagreement at the moment concerning the relationship between language and thought. In the writer's judgement the overall evidence tends to support the Piagetian viewpoint. In a longitudinal study of children Moore (93) obtained ratings on various aspects of the language development at 6 and 18 months, 3, 5 and 8 years, and intercorrelated these measures both among themselves and with general ability, both within and between ages. The evidence suggests that language may play a more important part in the early mental development of girls than in boys, yet even in the case of girls it did not appear to be a necessary condition of intellectual development.

FURTHER READING

Clark, H. H. and Begun, J. S. 'The Use of Syntax in Understanding Sentences', *Brit. J. Psychol.*, **59**, 219–29 (1968)

Dineen, F. P. *An Introduction to General Linguistics,* chapter 12 gives a useful introduction to transformational grammar (New York, Holt, Rinehart and Winston 1967)

Flavell, J. H. *et al. The Development of Role Taking and Communication Skills in Children* (London, Wiley 1968)

Herriot, P. 'The Experimental Psychology of Grammar and its Relevance to Children's Language Learning', *Development in Learning* 2 (Eds. Lunzer, E. A. and Morris, J. F.) (London, Staples 1968)

Inhelder, B. and Piaget, J. *The Early Growth of Logic in the Child,* Introduction and chapters 3 and 4 (London, Routledge and Kegan Paul 1964)

Kohlberg, L., Yaeger, J. and Hjertholm, E. 'Private Speech: Four Studies and a Review of Theories', *Child Developm.*, **39**, 691–736 (1968)

Lewis, M. M. *Language Thought and Personality in Infancy and Childhood* (London, Harrap 1963)

Lewis, M. M. 'Language and Mental Development', *Development in Learning* 2 (Eds. Lunzer, E. A. and Morris, J. F.) (London, Staples 1968)

Luria, A. R. and Yudovich, F. I. A. *Speech and the Development of Mental Processes in the Child* (London, Staples Press 1959)

McNeill, D. in *Psycholinguistic Papers*, pages 99–132 (Edinburgh, The University Press 1966)

Roberts, P. *English Syntax* (New York, Harcourt Brace 1964)

Sampson, O. For a series of papers relating speech with other variables between 18 months and 10 years of age, and involving a longitudinal study of children, see: *Brit. J. Educ. Psychol.*, 1956, **26**, 194–201; 1959, **29**, 217–22; 1962, **32**, 12–17; 1964, **34**, 143–50

Stott, L. H. *Child Development*, chapter 9 (London, Holt, Rinehart and Winston 1967)

Todd, G. A. and Palmer, B. 'Social Reinforcement of Infant Babbling', *Child Developm.*, **39**, 591–96 (1968)

5 The Development and Organisation of Personality

The term personality has been defined in many ways. The definition given here is that proposed by Allport (2): 'personality is the dynamic organisation within the individual of those psychophysical systems that determine his characteristic behaviour and thought'. This suggests in simpler language that personality is the whole of a person's outstanding characteristics, his physiology, drives, levels of aspiration, emotional and social traits, interests, attitudes and the like. It is not suggested that this definition is an adequate one, but it does at least allow the reader to grasp the complexity of the issues involved in any treatment of the development and organisation of personality.

Theories of personality attempt to explain how personality becomes organised or structured. A good theory should be able to account for the following: (1) the development of personality, (2) the functioning of personality in day to day situations, (3) both personality change and consistency throughout life. No theory has yet been propounded which will account for all the known facts, and it seems that such a theory remains a long way off. The many theories that have been proposed can for present purposes be divided into three broad kinds, namely, trait, developmental and dynamic theories. There are other kinds of theories but they are likely to be of less interest to the teacher.

TRAIT THEORIES

These will be discussed very briefly for while they are very helpful from the point of view of the organisation and description of personality, some do not emphasise sufficiently for the teacher, the developmental aspects. The work of R. B. Cattell is, perhaps, an exception as we shall see later. In essence trait theory describes a person on a number of scales; for example, introversion-extraversion. Those who use a trait theory approach do not altogether ignore the development aspects of personality although some point out how complicated these aspects are. Thus Allport (2) argues that the present motives now operating in the individual and directing his behaviour may not be the ones that were first responsible for that behaviour. For example, a young person may have commenced to smoke because the other members of his peer group were doing so; later he smokes because he enjoys it. However, quite apart from this difficulty, traits manifest themselves somewhat differently depending upon the environmental situation and how the individual subjectively perceives the situation. Indeed, personality characteristics do change somewhat according to the group in which we find ourselves or according to the roles we see ourselves playing. Thus a child may show a rather different personality structure with one teacher than with another. So it seems that we need some kind of interactive theory which takes into account the attributes that the individual possesses and the range of situations he is called upon to meet.

DEVELOPMENTAL THEORIES

It will be appreciated that our personality is organised or structured through various influences: heredity, experiences and training in infancy and childhood, and social motives acquired through learning. While individuals do go through certain common experiences common to all people in a particular culture, each person also has a unique set of experiences. Developmental theories may be conveniently divided into four groups: (1) psychoanalytic, (2) learning, (3) role, and (4) the concept of the self.

1. The classical psychoanalytic theory of Freud (41, 47) posits a theory of psychosexual development to explain personality organisation. In the first year of life the child passes through an *oral* stage where pleasure is obtained through lips and mouth, through sucking, swallowing and biting. If the child is not severely frustrated in his relationships with his mother or mother substitute

during this period, it is said that sound foundations are laid for his capacity to form stable relationships with other persons. The second year of life is characterised by the *anal* stage of personality development where pleasure is obtained through the expulsion and retention of faeces and through exercising the associated muscular control. Frustration at this stage, especially in connection with bowel training, is said to lead to an obstinate, compulsive character (retention) or to a disorderly and destructive character (expulsive). On the other hand it is argued that favourable experience during this period could lead to a creative and productive personality. Between the third and fifth year the source of pleasure changes again. It is now derived through genital stimulation and the functions which are associated with the genital area. The child becomes jealous of the special relationship between father and mother, and at the same time the boy becomes interested in his mother and the girl in her father. The individual is now at the *phallic-Oedipus* phase of development. The Oedipus jealousy may be helped by showing the child that while there is a special bond between father and mother, he is not rejected. As the Oedipus issue is resolved the child identifies with his parents, that is, he incorporates some of their qualities into his personality. The process of identification is an important one in the growth of personality organisation and will be enlarged upon later in this chapter. Finally we might note that it is during this phase that the child increasingly develops appropriate roles for his age and sex.

In the Freudian view there is a *latency* period from about the sixth to the twelfth year. Sexual interests *per se* seem to be repressed and the main source of pleasure comes from the child's interaction with the external world. Gratifications are now obtained through obtaining knowledge and through satisfying his curiosity about the world. This brings about the delightful child of junior school years, but for the child himself it is a most important period for he is acquiring basic knowledge and skills which enable him to cope with his environment. Finally in adolescence and adulthood the individual passes into the *genital* phase. He moves away from the self-love of the oral, anal, and phallic phases, also from the dependence upon parents, to a greater concern for others and to a position where pleasure is derived from the genital organs and from sexual relations with a partner of the opposite sex.

The Freudian conceptual framework is weak in dealing with the latency period, and perhaps does not deal adequately with the adjustments which the individual has to make in relationship to his environment and other persons. Moreover it has been pointed out that that the stages Freud proposes may be brought about by child-rearing practices within Western culture and may not be found universally. Erickson has proposed a theory which takes into account social and environmental conditions, although much of what he has to say seems likely to be of particular importance to the interacting subcultures of the United States of America.

2. All learning theories, whether they deal with the acquisition of knowledge and skills or with the growth and organisation of personality, look to those specific experiences of reward and punishment that shape development. Indeed the rewards and punishments that are given by persons who are of consequence and significance to the child are believed to be of great importance in forming habits. Both psychoanalytic and learning theories explain the present personality in terms of the past. In the latter type of theory, when the child meets a new situation he tends to deal with it in a manner much the same as he has dealt with rather similar situations in the past. If a particular experience has been enjoyable or frightening in the past, the new situation although not quite the same, will likewise produce a state of pleasure or fear as the case may be.

An extremely influential theory of learning has been elaborated by Hull who had, in turn, been influenced by the work of I. P. Pavlov and E. L. Thorndike. Readers will be aware that when food is placed in the mouth of a hungry dog, saliva usually begins to flow. But Pavlov showed in the early years of this century that saliva also flowed when the dog heard a bell (the conditioned stimulus) sounded immediately prior to the food being given. The dog had learned to associate the sound of the bell with the food soon to be eaten. This advanced flow of saliva was termed the conditioned response. The learning took place because of reinforcement, reward or drive-reduction, that is to say, food was always given after the bell was sounded and the drive for food was reduced.

Thorndike was also working with animals at about the same time. His experiments led him to the view that responses that are accompanied or closely followed by satisfaction are more likely to happen again when the situation recurs, while responses accompanied or closely followed by discomfort will be less likely to recur. This was known as the Law of Effect. In 1935 C. L. Hull suggested (57) that Pavlov's findings could be looked upon as a special instance of Thorndike's Law of Effect. He elaborated (58) a theory of learning which, while resting on much experimental evidence, was also firmly based on the principle that reinforcement, reward or drive-reduction (as when pain is reduced by escaping from a noxious stimulus) was central to all learning. Also central to his system was the notion of habit; the association of stimulus and response under reinforcement being the qualitative condition for habit strengthening. Hull's learning theory – although not the only one – has had great influence and it was necessary to give the barest elements of his ideas as they are of relevance for what immediately follows. Another book in this series will explain in much greater detail how learning theories stress the build up of habits which can be generalised into new situations.

Some learning theorists in the field of personality development have taken Freudian themes as a starting point and translated them, as it were, into terms of learning theory. This has been done by Whiting and Child (135); also Dollard and Miller (27). The last sentence does not imply, however, that any of these writers is necessarily committed to a psychoanalytic interpretation of personality.

Dollard and Miller use the concepts of habit, primary drive and secondary drive as essential parts of the structure of personality and which provide the stability for the personality organisation. By the term habit they mean a link which develops between a stimulus and the response which the subject makes to it, while the term drive implies a stimulus strong enough to impel the individual into action. There are primary drives, usually dependent upon physiological processes such as hunger, thirst, sex; and learned or secondary drives such as, say, ambition or fear, which, it is said, can be shown to arise from primary drives. It is the learned drives that play so large a part in instigating and controlling the behaviour of modern man.

On this view learning consists essentially of developing efficient means of reducing these drives. A certain response following a given stimulus is rewarding if the response reduces the drive which is operating at that time. If the response frequently follows that stimulus, then a habit is formed. But habits once formed may weaken or disappear as a result of absence of reward. Furthermore, the concept of generalisation is, as we saw a little earlier, given to the tendency to make the same response even although the stimulus changes somewhat. Thus a habit persists to new situations which bear similarity to old ones; for example, a child learns to exhibit similar behaviours of a helping nature to persons who are blind, deaf, or have lost limbs. At the same time, however, the child must also learn to respond differently to situations which are somewhat the same. For example, a child must learn to behave somewhat differently to a boy who is the same age but his brother, than to one of similar age but not of his family. Thus by rewarding one stimulus but not rewarding one very much like it, the individual learns to discriminate and cut down the tendency to generalise.

Consider again the concept of fear. This is said to be a learned response since a certain stimulus (e.g. the presence of some animal) which produces fear in one child will not do so in, say, a younger or more naïve one. But fear also acts as a drive in the sense that it will impel the individual to a certain form of activity (e.g. run away), while the reduction of the drive will reward the response of running away. Thus the learning principles which govern the formation of habits are also responsible for the acquisition of new motives.

Miller and Dollard contend that the early events of life are of paramount importance in personality development and that the learning of habits and motives take place in terms of the theory briefly described above. Four areas where events are said to have great effect on future personality development are: feeding in infancy, toilet training, early sex training, and control of sex and aggression. For example, if feeding is followed by gratification and drive reduction, the child will link this pleasant state with the mother. Moreover, because of stimulus generalisation he will have similar feelings for others.

Thus on the basis of learning theory Dollard and Miller explain the acquisition of habits and learned drives, and hence of the growth and organisation of personality. While they would argue that the principles of learning would apply in all cultures, they would also insist that the actual habits and motives acquired, and hence the behaviours displayed, are markedly influenced by the society in which the individual is reared.

3. A third theory of personality development is supplied by role theory. It will be dealt with briefly. An infant is born in a certain place so he has no say in respect of his choice of country or native language. In other matters he may be able to make a number of role choices. While the culture pattern may place restraints on these choices, the individual can, nevertheless, show his personality development through the consistency with which he plays the roles which he may or must play. In a complex society a person may have to play a number of roles, and the behaviour that he displays in each role depends upon the position that society has established for that role. Even in the simplest societies there are, according to Linton (74), at least five kinds of position. These are: age-sex; occupation; household or family; place in the hierarchy of rulers and ruled; and group membership based on common interests or skills (e.g. hunter, musician). A person occupying a certain position and playing the appropriate role must show some forms of behaviour, may show others, but must not show a third group of behaviours. Personality thus develops in terms of the consistency with which the individual learns to show characteristic features in his role behaviour.

4. Another developmental theory of personality is that which revolves around the concept of the self. Hall and Lindzey (48) have pointed out that the term does not yet have an agreed meaning and they have indicated some representative views which are held in respect of the self and the ego. Hilgard (53, 54) makes a useful distinction between the *inferred self* or the self judged by others competent to do so, and the *known self* or the self of which

the subject is personally aware. We shall keep to this division although it must be stressed that the concept of the self has not yet been fully assimilated into psychology.

The inferred self is sometimes referred to as the ego, although the term used in this way is not synonomous with the term used by Freud. It is the self as seen in making decisions and in planning in everyday life situations. Moreover the observer may recognise through defence mechanisms, unconscious forces at work of which the individual is quite unaware.

Our known self develops out of maturation and experience; it is essentially a product of an interactive process. The baby slowly differentiates his body from the objects that are around him, and the self-awareness of the position of his body serves as a main base for further experience and for the location of other objects. Moreover, the consistency of treatment he gets from his mother and from other persons close to him, the experience of warmth and comfort or of rejection, are all important influences in shaping the self. And by about the second birthday the child finds out if he is boy or girl and that certain ways of behaving are expected of him because of this.

With the coming of language the growth of the self is accelerated. The child, his toys, his playmates, his parents and so on are now all placed in certain categories, for the use of adjectives necessarily implies value judgements on the part of others, e.g. 'you are a little girl', 'this is a large red car'. Language also enables the growing self to relate itself to persons and objects not actually present, also to more abstract ideas connected with, say, virtue, ability, religion, art. As the child's width of experience increases his self attitudes are formed in relation to teacher, school, church, games, peer groups and the like, through participating in various relevant activities and noting the reactions of others to him and the language they use to describe his behaviour. It is true, of course, that intellectual growth plays a part in the build-up of the self. For example, the assessment of one's capacity in relation to other children when competing with them, and in setting consistent goals which at the same time are appropriate, do depend upon the growth of the intellect and are often beyond the powers of the young and the subnormal.

So the child comes to think of himself in such terms as: 'I am a girl', 'I am a good runner', 'I do not read as well as other children'. These positions which the child takes in respect of himself are known as self-attitudes. Such tend to make the child's behaviour more consistent, for he deals with situations more in terms of the claims that he makes about himself and becomes less affected by the immediate stimuli in the environment. Putting this in another way we can say that his major self-attitudes are responsible for determining, in some measure, those aspects of the environment to which he pays attention. Once again, because of this, the attitudes tend to bring relative consistency to our behaviour. It is important for the teacher to realise that he or she plays a part in shaping these self-attitudes and so in affecting the development of personality. A remark such as 'Susan is no good at arithmetic', made repeatedly and heard by the girl, is likely to produce a negative self-attitude in the girl. Even a remark such as 'Tom you cannot reach the shelf, you are not tall enough', which is meant to be harmless as far the teacher is concerned, can, if the essence of it is said enough times, markedly affect the child's picture of himself. So the child learns to see himself in relation to other people.

The known self is also seen as being responsible for our behaviour. I think that 'I' decide what I do although observers may think the behaviour is predetermined. The self is also seen as being continuous in time so that the past, present, and projections into the future, are all linked. This enables the self to reflect on its own worth – on its successes and failures – and because of this sense of continuity the maintenance of the picture of the self is of permanent concern to the individual. Finally, we must note that a system of values is built up around objects, persons and situations (e.g. honesty), so there develops the picture of the *ideal self* or the person we would like to be. These values can arouse emotions which enhance or degrade, respectively, the known self, when we behave in ways that are in keeping, or at variance, with them.

Overall we may say that the concept of the self is for some (e.g. Rogers 107) an important factor in determining the social behaviour of a person and in the development of the personality.

The definition of the self given by Sherif and Sherif (113) and stated below, although not distinguishing between the inferred self and the known self, does bring out a little of the argument we have developed: 'a developmental formation (a subsystem) in the psychological make up of the individual consisting of interrelated attitudes which are acquired in relation to his own body, to objects, family persons, groups, social values and institutions, and which define and regulate his relatedness to them in concrete situations.'

It is worth noting that mental ill health seems to arise when the gaps, as it were, between the ideal self and the known self, or between the known self and inferred self, are large.

DYNAMIC THEORIES

Dynamic theories of personality are greatly concerned with the present conflicts of the individual and how these may be resolved. They are, therefore, essentially interactive rather than developmental theories *per se*, although it must be remembered that the conflicts and the means to deal with them have developed out of the past whether as a result of constitutional or experiential influences. One interesting dynamic theory of personality is that proposed by Freud (41, 47). In his view personality may be thought of in terms of the interaction of three major components – the ID, EGO and SUPEREGO. The id, which is almost wholly within the unconscious mind, consists of instinctual drives; it knows neither values nor morality, it is non-rational and demands immediate satisfaction, and it is essentially pleasure loving. When a child acts on an impulse and throws a stone through a window he is under the control of the id. Similarly when he is constantly daydreaming he is under the domination of the id. The id does not think nor is it under the control of reason; it only acts or wishes.

But impulsive behaviour and wish fulfilment is not sufficient to ensure the survival of the human race. So a further psychological component termed the ego is necessary to order the relationship between the person and the outside world. The ego is broadly what we call consciousness, reason, sanity or will; it controls both the id and the superego (see later) so that it holds a balance between the strivings for satisfaction of the former, the censures of the latter, and the realities of the world. If the ego does not function efficiently and yields up too much of its power to the id, superego or the outside world, disharmony and maladjustment will result. For Freud the ego is largely a product of the inter-action of nature and nurture; the potentialities for thinking and reasoning are inborn, but education and experience of life are necessary for their realisation.

The third component of the personality is the superego. It grows out of the ego through the child's assimilations of his parents' standards regarding what is good and what is evil. Parents reward their children for certain kinds of conduct, so these forms of behaviour tend to become ideals for their children. Likewise children learn what their parents feel is morally bad through punishment. But two further points must be noted. It is what parents say and what they reward, rather than what they do that is important in this connection. The child's superego is a reflection of the parental superego and not of parental actions. Second, not only parents but grandparents, close relatives, teachers, peer groups, policemen and other agents of society, all contribute to the building of the superego, although the child's reactions to these other authority figures are largely determined by what he has assimilated earlier from his parents.

It will, of course, be appreciated that the id, ego and superego do not exist as separate, real entities, and signify nothing in them-selves. They merely provide a conceptual framework inside which we can discuss differing functions of the total personality.

In the Freudian view personality development takes place as a result of both maturation and of learning how to reduce anxiety, resolve conflicts, and overcome frustration. A child may be frustrated because the object or person he wants may be withheld or taken away, because what he wants is not to be found in the environment at the moment, or because there is a checking force acting in opposition to an urge. In the last condition there is conflict. Again frustration may be due to fear in the sense that the person is afraid to follow the goal he desires. Freud used the term anxiety rather than fear as the former term could include not only fear of something in the external world (e.g. wild animal or darkness) but also fear originating in the person himself (e.g. fear of some strong instinctual drive such as sex). It is the way in which the growing child meets and adjusts to these frustrations, conflicts and anxieties that shape the personality, and some of the methods used to accomplish this are now listed.

Identification

This is the incorporation of the qualities of another person into one's personality. Some types of identification grow out of frustration and anxiety and profoundly affect the growing personality. For example, a frustrated person will identify with a successful one in order to be successful himself. Thus a boy will grow more like his father in individual qualities (not as a whole person) if the father is attaining goals that the child desires. Again, if a child cannot possess, or has lost, an object which he desires he will try to make himself like that object. Thus a child who feels himself rejected by his parents will try to identify with what he thinks parents want him to be. A further kind of identification takes place in respect of parental restraints, teachers and other authority figures, in order to avoid punishment.

Displacement

The process by which an instinctual drive is diverted from one goal to another which is usually more socially acceptable, is called displacement. Such a change of goal, on this theory is a major influence in personality development. The culture pattern, mediated through parents and teachers, will influence the direction the displacement will take. For example, individuals require a certain amount of oral gratification and in the baby this is satisfied by sucking at the nipple. In childhood the instinctual drive is diverted to thumbsucking, and licking a lollipop. The former activity is usually discouraged but the latter is not except perhaps by the dentist on account of dental caries. But in the adult licking a lollipop would be regarded as strange if done frequently, although licking an icecream would not be so regarded and sucking a pipe would be completely acceptable. The displacement is called a sublimation if the substitute objects represent a higher cultural goal, so that the energy associated with, say, the sex and aggressive instincts are deflected into cultural and intellectual pursuits. Freud was of the opinion that sublimation did not result in complete satisfaction and that the remaining tension was in part responsible for the nervousness of civilised man. But he also regarded sublimation as responsible for man's highest cultural achievements.

Ego defence mechanisms

In its efforts to overcome the conflicts between the id, superego and the real world, the ego sometimes tries to alleviate anxiety by means which distort or falsify reality and hold back the growth of the personality (40). One of the methods used is known as *repression*. Sometimes there are 'built in' barriers resulting from experience of the race which keep certain contents of the id permanently in the unconscious. For example, there seems to be a universal prohibition against incest. But more generally the ego will force an idea, memory or perception out of consciousness if it engenders great anxiety so that, for example, memories which involve traumatic experiences are repressed and cannot be brought to mind except under rather special circumstances. Another mechanism used by the id is *projection* which implies the thrusting forth on to other persons, unconscious ideas and wishes that would provoke anxiety if accepted as part of the self. Projection is said to take place frequently in children's play, as when, say, in doll-play they often express their unconscious needs and desires.

It is the manner in which the child uses these and other defence mechanisms to handle day-to-day conflicts that results in the personality organisation and renders behaviour relatively consistent. These mechanisms do deny and distort reality to some extent and thus they tend to hinder psychological growth. If a particular mechanism becomes strong it can dominate the ego and reduce its capacity for flexibility in tackling the conflicts which everyone encounters in life. Moreover, if the defence mechanisms break down, the individual is likely to be overwhelmed with anxiety.

Learning theory also deals with conflicts in personality development. But here the concepts employed are habits and drives rather than id, ego and superego. Likewise when a person has to play a number of roles, conflicts may be produced when he has to overcome these by new habits or a new range of behaviours.

Mention was made earlier of the developmental theory of Erickson which is also a dynamic one. His work is firmly rooted in Freudian analytic concepts but at the same time he advances far beyond Freud. Erickson (30, 31, 32, 33) takes less interest in the id and places more emphasis on the ego; he considers the individual in a wide social setting; and he places great value on overcoming psychological and social conflicts and crises for such victories are conducive to further development. He has divided the life span up into a number of phases, but we shall here consider only the first five, that is, up to and including the period of adolescence. Whether Erickson's phases are to be found universally, or whether they have particular relevance to conditions in the USA today is a matter which needs discussing although it will not be argued here.

Phase I. Acquiring a sense of basic trust.

In Erickson's view this is the most fundamental phase as it lays the foundation for the personality development that follows. In infancy the child needs to experience a minimum of fear and uncertainty and a large measure of physical comfort and care. A sense of basic trust develops which enables the child to grow psychologically and look forward, with favourable expectations, to new experiences.

Phase 2. Acquiring a sense of autonomy and overcoming a sense of doubt and shame.

This phase lasts roughly from 18 months to 4 years of age. Within the security given by mother and home, the child establishes that his behaviour belongs to him, that is, he develops a sense of autonomy. But he is also aware that he is still dependent upon his environment – physical, psychological and social – and this makes him doubt if he can be autonomous thereby engendering a sense of doubt and shame. At this time the child needs careful guidance and support, the latter carefully graded to help him develop his sense of autonomy. Erickson believes that the way control is exercised over the child's behaviour during this period affects his ideals in later life and his attitudes to society.

Phase 3. Acquiring a sense of initiative and overcoming a sense of guilt.

To the child between four and seven years of age the world is an exciting and adventurous place for he is at an inquisitive stage and wants to explore and find out about his environment. A sense of initiative runs through his life. At the same time, however, the autonomy he has acquired is now often frustrated by the autonomous behaviour of others. Moreover he learns that the adults who are round about him do not always care as did those he encountered in his earlier life. As a result he experiences some sense of guilt and a desire to withdraw from frustrating situations. But withdrawal increases his sense of guilt, since he denies his own desires to explore and exploit the opportunities in the exciting world about him. This conflict between initiative, and either passivity or guilt, for living too adventurously or too weakly respectively compared with his inner desires, is for Erickson the crucial feature of these years. Homes, nursery and primary schools, can help the child by pointing out the range of initiative possible for him at this stage of development.

Phase 4. Acquiring a sense of industry and keeping off a sense of inferiority.

The pupil, now in junior school, or the child in the hours out of school, puts a very great deal of his energy into learning by doing, and developing the basic skills of his culture. Opposed to this is the fear that he is still an incomplete person. So at this phase we have a sense of industry versus a sense of inferiority. The child now begins to identify with other adults, for his parents no longer have all the attributes that the child demands of his models. Moreover, by the end of this period, peers are needed for the purpose of maintaining his own self-esteem and as a measuring rod against which he can judge his own success and failure. He also identifies with his peers.

Phase 5. Acquiring a sense of identity.

This phase corresponds broadly with the period of adolescence. The young person is now asking questions such as 'Which way can I be?', for a sense of identity is necessary before decisions in respect of, say, future work can be made. Knowledge of who he is in the present and who he is going to be in the future, gives him confidence in himself and paves the way for future development. Now he needs assurance from his peer group, members of which are also in a state of change. Indeed, peer relationships are an essential authority in enabling one to determine one's identity. Erickson considers that the period of adolescence is a most valuable one in that it provides the young person with opportunities to experiment with different identities before he makes any final decisions.

In considering the many theories of personality development that have been outlined it is important not to lose sight of constitutional influences. Thus in connection with the University of California's longitudinal studies Bronson (14) showed that the dimensions of withdrawal-expressiveness and reactivity-placidity did not seem to be modifiable over the age range five to sixteen. It would appear that constitutional influences are at work. But the dimension of passivity-dominance seemed to be more a product of organismic qualities and psychosocial pressures.

A psychologist who has not ignored heredity and other constitutional influences is R. B. Cattell (22). Unfortunately he uses rather complex terminology and his views will only be briefly given here. Cattell draws heavily upon psychoanalaytic and learning theory but in addition he introduces his own concepts. One of these is the ERG. By this he means a kind of innate drive directed to some particular goal, e.g. sexual goal, although he insists that the term erg is not synonymous with drive. The latter has, in Cattell's view, no precise meaning, whereas erg can be defined more exactly since it is derived from a statistical analysis of data obtained from many different behaviours of the same persons. He lists as ergic goals: curiosity, sex, protection, gregariousness, self-assertion, security, hunger, anger, disgust, appeal and self-submission. As Cattell himself says, this list is strikingly like those provided by McDougall, Lorenz and Tinbergen through studying the natural behaviour of higher animals. In Cattell's view, one attitude leads on to a second which leads on to a third and so on until ultimately one of the ergic goals is reached. Thus we work hard at our studies, to pass an examination, to obtain a good job, to earn enough money, to be able to marry and to be free of hunger. While our behaviour at the first level (working hard) might be explained in terms of a simple motive, in reality all our attitudes lead to ergic goals.

In addition, social and cultural factors and everyday experience of life bring about *sentiments*, which for Cattell, indicate sets of attitudes the strength of which has become correlated through their being all learnt by conduct with a particular person or social situation. He also uses the concept of *self-sentiment*. By this means the individual acquires the ability to contemplate the physical and social self, so that the satisfaction of any desire is considered in relation to the sentiment for the welfare of the whole self. This, the self-sentiment, controls all the other sentiments to some degree. Thus Cattell writes (22, p. 272): 'Dynamically, the sentiment towards maintaining the self correct by certain standards of conduct, satisfactory to community and super-ego, is therefore a necessary instrumentality to the satisfaction of most other of our life interests'. So for Cattell the development of personality consists in the modification of ergs through teaching training and general experience of life; the build up of attitudes, interests and sentiments; and the organisation of the self-sentiment.

FURTHER READING

Allport, G. W. *Pattern and Growth in Personality*, chapters 1–16 (New York, Holt Rinehart and Winston 1961)

Baldwin, A. L. *Theories of Child Development*, chapters 10–17 and 19 (London, Wiley 1967)

Biddle, B. J. and Thomas, E. J. *Role Theory: Concepts and Research* (London, Wiley 1966)

Blum, G. S. *Psychoanalytic Theories of Personality* (London, McGraw Hill 1953)

Cattell, R. B. *Introduction to Personality Study* (London, Hutchinson 1950)

Cattell, R. B. *Personality and Motivational Structure and Measurement*. A more difficult book. Chapters 11–13 (New York, World Book Co. 1957)

Combs, A. W. and Snygg, D. *Individual Behaviour* (New York, Harper 1949)

Hutt, M. L., Isaacson, R. L. and Blum, M. L. *Psychology: The Science of Interpersonal Behaviour*, chapters 2, 3, 5 (London, Harper and Row 1967)

McCary, J. L. (Ed.) *Psychology of Personality: Six Modern Approaches* (New York, Logos Press 1956)

Maier, H. W. *Three Theories of Child Development*, chapters 2, 4, 5 (New York, Harper and Row 1966)

Murphy, G. *Personality* (New York, Harper and Row 1947)

Sarnoff, I. *Personality Dynamics and Development* (London, Wiley 1962)

Wiggins, J. 'Personality Structure', *Annual Review of Psychology*, 19 (Palo Alto, Annual Reviews Inc. 1968)

6 The Social Context of Personality Development

In the previous chapter we dealt with general theories of personality development and organisation. Now we are going to discuss in more detail the social context of this development.

Every society has to SOCIALISE its young. By this term it is indicated that the child, considered biologically, has to be brought to the position where he behaves in a way appropriate to his place in that society. He has to learn how to control his impulses or natural tendencies, and to attain the many basic skills, both interpersonal and technical, necessary for him to take his place in that society bearing in mind his age and sex. In all societies much of this is done without formal teaching although in no society are things left entirely to chance. In societies other than the simplest ones, the school plays a considerable part in this process. At the outset it must be stressed that anthropologists and sociologists have made many studies of the patterns of arrangements made for socialising the child, but far fewer of the effects of these patterns on child behaviour.

CULTURAL INFLUENCES

It is now well realised that the culture pattern in which a child is brought up does shape the developing personality even although we do not know its exact effects. The work of Malinowski (87) and Mead (88, 89) showed the great variability of behaviour in different cultures, so what had been thought of as essential 'human behaviour' was shown to be the product of the particular culture pattern in which the individual was reared. There are many reasons why both culture, and variables specific to a society, should be taken into account in attempting to estimate the effect of socialisation procedures. In the first place it is difficult within a single society to distinguish the effects on the child of other people's behaviour and the meaning the child gives to these behaviours. For example, was the hostility of sons towards their fathers which Freud observed due to the fact that the father was the disciplinarian or his mother's lover? A comparative study between such a society and another where the boy's uncle is the disciplinarian should elucidate this issue. Second, although we cannot define the phrase 'child-rearing practices' precisely – in a general way it means all the interactions between parents and their children – it is important to try to find out if given child-rearing practices are only effective with certain other conditions existing within the cultural context. Third, the range of behaviours found in any one cultural context is limited. But having made a case for cross cultural studies of socialisation practices it must also be said that the behaviour of individuals will never be predictable from culture alone. There will always remain individual differences in biological make up and hence in temperament; cultural impacts on the child will always come through particular people who have their own specific set of behaviours and practices; while each child will have his own unique experiences. Additional reasons will be given later.

An as example of the likely effects of cultural influences consider the views of Whiting and Whiting (136). They point out that the composition of the household may have important implications for personality development. In Western societies most families are of the nuclear type, that is, they consist of father, mother and unmarried children. In other societies we may find the extended family in which married children and their spouses also live with the parents and the unmarried children. A third arrangement involves communal households where up to perhaps thirty families sleep; while in yet other societies there is the mother-child household in which father sleeps either in a hut or in the men's house. It seems likely that these differing arrangements must affect the personality development of the child. First, the number of adults in intimate contact with any one child and with whom he is likely to identify, varies with the type of household. And, in the mother-child household, there is no father with whom the boy can identify so that some societies have found it necessary

G

to have definite means, perhaps through some marked initiation ceremony, of changing the object of the boy's identification before adulthood. Second, the number of people in the household and the amount of physical space available, are likely to influence the timing, the methods used, and the values felt important to transmit to the child during the socialisation process. In an extended family, weaning and training for independence are likely to come later than in a nuclear family since a number of children are not competing for the attention of one woman. Again in the extended family there is likely to be greater prohibition of aggression than in the nuclear family while the methods used to inhibit aggression must be subdued and unobtrusive. In the former type family there is also a greater tendency to feel responsibility to the group, whereas the nuclear family puts more emphasis on self-reliance. But the exact outcomes, from the point of view of personality development, of these differing types of household are not known.

The now well-known studies of Mead (89) showed that among the Arapesh – a nonliterate people of New Guinea – infants received much affection and indulgent handling. As adults they were a generous and optimistic people. On the other hand the Mundugumor, who are of the same stock as the Arapesh, showed little affection in handling their children who grew up into impatient and quarrelsome adults. At the same time Campbell (21) found that although the children of a West Indian island were treated with great affection in infancy, they nevertheless grew up into insecure and suspicious adults. From these and other studies it can be seen that the relationship between handling in infancy and later behaviour is complex. While it may be claimed that the nature of such a handling does affect personality, it is not the only influence at work. Later influences in childhood may correct earlier training, or they may continue to thwart and frustrate the child.

So far it has been assumed that perhaps child-rearing practices are the cause and antecedents of personality and culture. But there is also evidence that child-rearing practices can be the product of certain aspects of the culture. For example, the Israeli collectives (kibbutzim) are a very good, even if extreme example, of methods of child-rearing determined by ideology and values.

EFFECTS OF DIFFERENT PATTERNS OF CHILD-REARING
WITHIN THE USA

The study of Sears, Maccoby and Levin (110) set out to establish
the child-rearing antecedents of certain kinds of fantasy behaviour
in five-year-old children. One important finding was that the warmth
of the mother's feeling for her child had a widespread beneficial
influence on behaviour. Obversely, coldness on the part of the
mother was associated with feeding problems and bedwetting.
Reward proved more effective than punishment in establishing
ways of behaving, and the authors insist that punishment is
ineffective, in the long run, as a technique for eliminating those
kinds of behaviour to which it is directed. The effect of permissiveness in child-rearing was not nearly so clear except in the case
of aggression. Here a permissive attitude to aggression encouraged
the child to express himself in aggressive fashion. However
because of the notion held in some quarters that child-rearing
practices are all-important for personality development, it is
worth stating that these authors conclude that constitution
variations provide the basis for the uniqueness of the personality growth and that personality is the product of many things
of which child-rearing experience is but one. Behaviour at any
time results from constitutional endowment, the personality
that has been developed to that point, and the immediate
situation. The child-rearing practices that a person undergoes
do not play a unique role in his personality development, but
introduce some effect at some stages in the person's growth.

Another relevant study is that of Sears, Rau and Alpert (111)
which investigated the effects of child-rearing on the identification process. Four types of parental behaviour were considered:
nurturance and warmth (desire for intimacy and affection, reward
of dependency); high demands (the encouragement of mature
forms of behaviour in respect of the control of aggression, demands for achievement, conformity to standards, good manners,
the taking of responsibility); love-orientated discipline (use of
praise, reasoning or putting into isolation, but no physical
punishment); use of models and labels (the former term relates
to the use of parents as models and the latter indicates a belief in

the importance of teaching the difference between right and wrong often necessitating the use of verbalisations). They also tested, at four years of age, the hypothesis that there should be substantial correlations between certain kinds of behaviour in girls but not in boys. The argument here was that both sexes identify with the mother originally. At four years of age certain behaviours should continue to cluster together in the girl but not in the boy, since somewhere between the second and fourth years the boy would begin identification with the father.

The results of the study broadly confirmed their hypothesis. In the girl, attention seeking, adult role behaviour, adult mannerisms, giving facts, emotional upset after wrongdoing, and femininity did form a cluster. But resistance to temptation did not form part of this group of behaviours. In boys, however, these traits had a median intercorrelation coefficient of about zero. Of the four types of child-rearing variables hypothesised as antecedents of the cluster of child behaviours, only high demands seemed to be generally correlated with it, although there did appear to be a slight linkage with the use of models and labels. The authors conclude that in the earliest years both sexes adopt feminine-maternal ways of behaving, but between two and four years of age the boy commences to shape his behaviour to that of the male role providing male models are available. Female characteristics then become displaced. But the attitudes of the parents towards the control of aggression and sex are more influential in determining masculinity and femininity than in the presence or the behaviour of models.

Schaefer and Bayley (109) in a longitudinal study, investigated the relationship between maternal behaviour and the social and emotional development of the children. The sample consisted of 27 boys and 27 girls from the Berkeley Growth Study. Maternal behaviour in relation to their children was assessed when the latter were between birth and 3 years of age, and again when they were between 9 and 14 years. The authors found that the most important dimension of maternal behaviour was that which they termed love-hostility or accepting-rejecting. Maternal behaviour over the years was consistent on this dimension; perhaps this is due to the fact that a child's need for a good relationship with the mother and the latter's capacity to give it are relatively stable. During the first three years of life maternal love was associated with children who were happy, calm, showed an interest in the environment, and made an effort when given a task. This was true of both sexes. The relationships between early maternal love and the social and emotional responses of boys then decreased although the correlations with interest and effort remained until twelve years of age. In the case of the girl, however, maternal love was related to child behaviour only until four years of age. Maternal behaviour between 9 and 14 years of age was significantly correlated with boys' behaviour at all the ages studied, but in the case of daughters such correlations were found only in adolescence. It seems that the boy's adjustment depends more on stable relationships built up through the years, whereas in the girl adjustment seems more dependent on her current interpersonal relationships. It is clear though that the effect of parental behaviour is different for boys than girls.

Bayley and Schaefer (8) suggest that over the first 18 years of life the measured intelligence of boys is related to the love-hostility dimension of maternal behaviour. The sons of hostile mothers showed lower IQs after four years of age, whereas the boys who showed a high level of intelligence throughout the years had loving mothers. In the case of girls maternal behaviour had little influence, and their IQs correlated highest with the education of their parents and the estimates of the mothers' IQ.

This longitudinal study has also shown that socio-economic conditions are more related to measured IQ than they are to social and emotional characteristics. This is in agreement with earlier research findings.

SOCIAL CLASS INFLUENCES

By social class is meant the manner in which people are ranked in the hierarchy of power and prestige. Now we have just seen that the effect of child-rearing practices and maternal behaviour on personality development is complex. More immediately apparent from the point of view of such development are the differences in patterns of authority and expectations for the child as between the social classes – especially between the extremes of the professional classes and unskilled workers. It must, however, be pointed out that any differences suggested below tend to decrease with the rise in standards of living and with better standards of education all round. Furthermore, it is not social class *per se* which is the important variable but rather, as stated already, middle class parents have different expectations for their children than do, say, unskilled workers.

Most parents, regardless of social class, do look to the future when considering the qualities they value for their children. But the varying social groups see their offspring playing different roles in adult life. Thus middle class parents and lower working-class parents differ in respect of the traits they want their children to develop in the present. American studies (e.g. Kohn 68) suggest that middle class parents emphasise internalised standards of conduct yielding self-control, while working class parents stress qualities that ensure respectability; e.g. obedience. Thus working class mothers tend to put more value on conformity to certain rules and judge a child's actions in terms of their immediate consequences, whereas middle class mothers tend to judge their child's actions in terms of feelings, intentions and motives (Kohn 69). It is also fair to say that among middle class parents there is a greater degree of permissiveness in respect of the child's needs and desires, but greater pressure is placed on the child in respect of a high level of performance in school work and achievement generally. So while we find greater freedom for the middle class child in respect of some aspects of his behaviour, much more is expected of him in other ways.

Two points, however, must be stressed. The statements made above are generalisations. Some working class parents do have middle class values in matters of behaviour and achievement; while some affluent families have two cars in the garage but few books in the home. Wiseman (137) has produced evidence that parental attitudes to education, to school and to books, are of more importance in respect of scholastic attainment in the primary school than are social class and educational level. He has also shown (137) among secondary school children that the quality of maternal care is of great importance to the attainment of children;

indeed it may be of much more importance than material needs. A quotation from the Plowden Report (Vol. 2, page 369) expresses the upshot clearly: 'The child from a home with an income of £20 per week may be more at risk than one from a much poorer home'.

The second point is that we do not know with any degree of exactitude what the long-term effects of these social class differences are on personality development (Sewell (112)). It seems that the differences outlined above do affect children's aspirations, attitudes and values. But we do not know with any certainty if more fundamental aspects of the personality are affected, such as the adjustment of the individual to life generally, although it is not implied that these aspects are not influenced at all. However, the fact that child attitudes and values are affected has profound implications for the teacher since, in general, these are reflected in performance at school. Indeed, pupils from the most economically and socially deprived groups often show lack of motivation in respect of school performance and a paucity of vocabulary and experience relevant to the materials and situations used by teachers in school. Perhaps the adults with whom such children could identify were poor models. Yet even here one must be very careful, for it is always possible to think of a child whose family was at best indifferent to scholastic performance, but who, nevertheless, made good progress in primary, secondary and higher education. Individual characteristics, good models, and opportunities in later childhood and adolescence, are all of value in personality development.

SEX ROLE AND PERSONALITY DEVELOPMENT

We have already seen that the age at which children recognise their sex has been well studied. But our knowledge of the effects of being a boy or a girl on personality development is more limited. It is, however, certain that the culture pattern affects the roles that male and female are expected to play.

In a study of over one hundred nonliterate societies, Barry *et al* (7) showed that in general (but not always) the more the economy of the society was dependent upon motor skills and physical strength, the greater were the differences in the upbringing of boys and girls. In infancy there were few differences, but in later childhood those societies which did differentiate between the sexes in child-rearing practices mainly followed what appears to be a common pattern: pressure on the boys to become self-reliant and to strive after achievement, and pressure on girls towards obedience and responsibility.

Kagan, Hoshen and Watson (62), also other workers, have shown that well before ten years of age children see the male as aggressive, competent, fear-arousing and less nurturant than the female. At least that is the position in the USA. A belief that aggression is more appropriate for men than women comes early in life and almost certainly contributes to the suppression of overt aggression in the girl. This suggestion is confirmed by a longitudinal study of 36 males and 35 females from birth to about 24 years of age undertaken by Kagan and Moss (63), who concluded that sex-role identification did play a major part in determining which behaviours will be adopted and maintained by the sexes over the years. It was found that behaviours which emerged in the six to ten-year-old period, and a few which emerged during the years between three and six, were moderately good predictors of related behaviours in early adulthood. If the young adult showed anxiety in social situations, striving for intellectual attainment, dependency on family, passive withdrawal from stressful situations, clear sex-role identification and a pattern of sexual behaviour, he or she also showed, apart from certain exceptions to be mentioned in a moment, related behavioural dispositions in the early school years. But in the case of both boys and girls certain behaviours (different for the two sexes) tend to disappear.

Kagan and Moss suppose that part of the ideal self consists of being an ideal male or an ideal female, and they suggest that the degree to which one expresses competitiveness, passivity, aggression, dependence and sexuality depends, in part, upon the individual's assessment of the degree of congruence of the behaviour with what is expected in terms of the cultural sex-role standards. Passive and dependent behaviour are disapproved of in boys, as are aggressive retaliation and frequent sexual behaviour in girls. The study indicated that aggressiveness and sexuality found in the behaviour of children continued when the boys became young adult males but not when the girls became young adult females. In other words it seems that the individual's desire to mould his behaviour in accordance with the expectations of the culture pattern is an important factor influencing his personality development.

It must also be remembered that sex-role values do change somewhat according to social class. Certain behaviours may be accepted in one social class more than in another.

In Chapter 1 it was pointed out that when the genotypic and phenotypic sex is inconsistent, most persons think of themselves as belonging to the sex which they represent or approach phenotypically. The sex given to a child by adults and confirmed in a multitude of ways in their day to day relationships with him determines the sex he will adopt. Moreover it seems that where surgical interference is necessary to reassign the child's sex in accordance with some biological function, serious psychological problems are almost inevitable for him unless the change is made before two years of age.

SOCIOLOGICAL ASPECTS OF THE FORMATION OF CERTAIN KINDS OF DEVIANT BEHAVIOURS

So far we have been dealing with what, from the sociological viewpoint, we might broadly call normal personalities. There is, however, in lower class urban areas, a considerable amount of delinquency. This is even truer of the USA than of Britain. Outlined below are three theories, elaborated in the USA to fit American conditions, which might have some relevance for this country. In essence they attempt to explain how subcultural conditions may explain the development of deviant behaviours or deviant personalities. Note carefully that such personalities may not be markedly deviant in a psychopathological sense. It must also be clearly understood that such theories do not take into account individual biological and psychological variations – caused by genetic, pre-, para- and postnatal conditions – which may also play a part in predisposing persons to develop deviant behaviours because of their reduced capacity to handle stressful situations (cf Stott, 119, 120).

Cohen (25) first proposed what has become known as the status-deprivation theory. In essence this claims that everyone is sensitive to the evaluations of others, especially those in authority. Inability to gain status, or loss of status, may mean a serious adjustment problem for some young people. Middle class values such as individual responsibility, skill, ambition, respect for property and so on are expected of everyone in a democracy regardless. But, in Cohen's view, social class differences in outlook coupled with differences in housing standards leave many youngsters ill equipped to measure up to and accept middle class values and standards. Because of this they are not held in high esteem by teachers and other representatives of authority which in turn leads to their losing their self-esteem. Boys who have an ambivalent attitude to middle class standards tend to form gangs, for such boys with adjustment problems must have a collective solution to the problem of defending themselves against middle class judgements. Hostility and resentment in respect of society then further develops. Thus Cohen describes the subculture as malicious, negativistic, and demanding the right to run their own lives free of all adult control.

Cloward and Ohlin (24) think somewhat differently. They argue that deviant personalities in delinquent subcultures arise from the fact that there are not the opportunities for advancement among children in the lower social classes. Boys who want only higher incomes and are not concerned with getting into a higher social class – and so do not seem to be concerned about middle class esteem – react against the unjust distribution of opportunity and become hostile to society. This is known as the opportunity-structure theory. The authors also predict that, according to the conditions existing in the neighbourhood, such alienation will lead to subcultures which display a level of stable crime, or are violent, or their members will indulge in marked withdrawal behaviour and drug taking.

A third point of view has been proposed by Miller (90). This does not subscribe to the theory that delinquent subcultures result from real or imagined deprivation within a society. Rather, the conditions of life are such in a competitive society, that those at the bottom of the economic ladder in urban areas (American) develop a distinctive culture of their own. The employment situation for adolescents in such circumstances is often difficult and the boys develop a longing for autonomy, excitement, smartness, toughness and trouble.

At present it is not possible to make tests which would be crucial in deciding the worth of these theories. Such theories by-pass three important influences likely to be of consequence in the development of personality and hence likely to affect its potential for delinquency. These influences are: The quality of the earlier relationships with the mother and other close adults which can give security and a sense of personal status to the child; the socialisation provided in the early years affecting qualities of character; the biological equipment of the child which makes it easier or more difficult to tolerate frustration.

MATERNAL DEPRIVATION AND PERSONALITY DEVELOPMENT

It is often difficult to know exactly what is meant by the term 'maternal deprivation' although much has been written about its effects on personality development. Yarrow (141) in an excellent view of the relevant literature discusses four kinds of deviation from what may be broadly called normal maternal care. These are: separation from a mother or mother substitute; distortion in the quality of mothering, e.g. ambivalence, rejection, over-protection; multiple mothering in which there is not one person consistently performing the functions normally performed by a mother; and institutionalisation.

There is some certain knowledge in this field, but there also remains much uncertainty in spite of the fact that many dogmatic statements have been made from time to time. Much of the research has lacked methodological rigour. However, it is known that severe sensory deprivation before the first birthday, if it continues long enough, can lead to marked failure in intellectual development. Again there is evidence that when very young children are separated from their mothers as in, say, a stay in hospital, many do show a variety of immediate disturbances in their behaviour suggesting that separation is a stressful situation for them.

On the other hand no clear cut conclusions can be drawn from the effects of institutionalisation, maternal separation, or distortions in the quality of mothering. Not all institutions are alike in the degree of deprivation they offer the child, because of constitutional differences not all children react in the same way to maternal separation, while the degree and type of distortion of mothering varies between mothers. Again, as Yarrow points out, it is not known how later experiences affect the position: they may act as reinforcing or attenuating influences as far as personality development is concerned. Moreover, there is no evidence that any personality damage results from multiple mothering provided that there is no associated deprivation or stress. Finally we do not know, at present, the extent to which language deprivation in early childhood can be made good by language enrichment programmes in later childhood.

The long term study of Skeels (115) suggests that the ill effects of institutionalisation can, at least in some instances, be overcome if action is taken very early in life. In 1939 he reported the effects on mental growth of a radical shift in environment by moving children from one institution to another. The children in question had come to the first institution – a very poor one – from homes which were at low social, economic, occupational and intellectual levels. In the second institution the children were able to have greater facilities for varied play, to receive greater intellectual stimulation, and to make warm personal relationships with older girls and members of staff. The children were aged between 7 and 30 months at the time of transfer. These, and a control group of children who were left in the first institution have been followed by Skeels after more than 20 years. He found that of the group who were transferred, every single one was self supporting and the occupational range was from professional to semi-skilled. The mean school grade completed was 11·5. In the case of the control group the mean school grade completed was 4; the members of the group, with one exception, were institutional inmates, dishwashers, persons frequently changing their jobs which were of an unskilled nature, and one part-time worker in a cafeteria. The exception was a man who had become a compositor and typesetter.

There were only small numbers of children involved in Skeels' study, but it does suggest that in some instances the worst effects of institutionalisation can be overcome if action is taken early enough. But if deprivation continues the outlook is not very promising, although even here one must be cautious. One of the deprived children in the control group did turn out to be a highly skilled workman. So before we can speak with certainty about maternal deprivation and personality development we need to know something of the child's constitutional characteristics, the exact nature of the deprivation, its intensity, and how long it continued. In addition we need to know far more about the extent to which the situation can be reversed if action is taken early enough.

FURTHER READING

Bandura, A. and Walters, R. H. *Social Learning and Personality Development* (New York, Holt, Rinehart and Winston 1963)

Blyth, W. A. L. 'Social Contexts of Development and Learning', *Development in Learning* 3 (Eds. Lunzer, E. A. and Morris, J. F.) (London, Staples 1969)

Casler, L. 'Maternal Deprivation: A Critical Review of the Literature', *Monogr. Soc. Res. Child Developm.*, 26 (2) (1961)

Freeberg, N. E. and Payne, D. T. 'Parental Influence on Cognitive Development in Early Childhood: A Review', *Child Developm.*, 38, 65–87 (1967)

Jensen, A. R. 'The Culturally Disadvantaged: Psychological and Educational Aspects', *Educ. Res.*, 10, 4–20 (1967)

Kaplan, B. (Ed.) *Studying Personality Cross Culturally* (New York, Harper and Row 1961)

Kohlberg, L. 'A Cognitive-Developmental Analysis of Children's Sex Role Concepts and Attitudes', *The Development of Sex Differences* (Ed. Macoby, E. E.) (London, Tavistock 1967)

Lindzey, G. (Ed.) *Handbook of Social Psychology*, chapter 17 (Reading, Mass., Addison-Wesley 1954)

Merrill, F. E. *Society and Culture*, chapters 7–10 (London, Prentice-Hall, 3rd Edition 1954)

Newcombe, T. M. and Hartley, E. L. (Ed.) *Readings in Social Psychology,* Parts III and VIII (New York, Henry Holt 1958)

Sargent, S . S. and Williamson, R. C. *Social Psychology,* chapter 6 (New York, Ronald Press 1966)

Schaffer, H. R. 'Social Learning and Identification', *Development in Learning* **2** (Eds. Lunzer, E. A. and Morris, J. F.) (London, Staples 1968)

World Health Organisation *Deprivation of Maternal Care: A Re-assessment of its Effects* (Public Health Papers, No. 14 1962)

7 Moral Development

Introduction

The term *morality* or *conscience* is today taken to indicate a set of rules for determining one's social actions and which have been internalised by the individual. But there are three points to be noted. First, the rules tend to be related to the culture so that what is moral in one society may not be in another. Second, rules are internalised if they are obeyed because of some inner motivation and not because of external incentives, threats or sanctions. Third, in psychological studies it is often difficult to separate morality from a study of values. But since Kant's time, at least, moral values have carried, within a culture, a sense of obligation so that the individual thinks 'I ought' or 'I should', whereas other values carry desirability. For example, aesthetic values are certainly not imperatives.

Having defined morality it is important to note that different studies of the acquisition of morality have emphasised different aspects of the problem. Hartshorne and May (51) investigated moral conduct and to a small extent the intellectual dimension of morality. For them morality was reflected in moral character displayed in situations that demanded honesty, service and self-control. Internal conformity was assessed by measuring the habits of children in temptation situations. Freud and his followers were more concerned with moral feeling. As we have already seen he posited the elaboration of a superego through identification with the parents. The superego brought about a sense of guilt for failure to resist temptation and a sense of shame for personal inadequacy; at the same time it enhanced self-esteem for either virtue or ability. The existence of internalised standards is, on this view, recognised by the presence of guilt, that is, self-punishing and self-critical reactions, after transgression of the rules. Then there is the intellectual or judgemental side of moral development which has been studied by Piaget (99) and more recently by Kohlberg (66, 67). It has been shown that there are stages of moral development, and it is said that the child is moral when he makes decisions of principle – appropriate to each stage – and says that he 'ought' to do so and so because he has made these principles his own. All three approaches are relevant to the problem of children's acquisition of morality. Unfortunately, as we know only too well from everyday life, there is only a modest correlation between moral judgements and moral conduct. It is not possible, however, to review the massive literature that surrounds the question of the acquisition of morality or conscience from the point of view of learning, psychoanalytic and role-learning theories. A few comments and conclusions about each will be given in turn.

LEARNING THEORY AND MORALITY

Learning theory in this context, as in many others, has been greatly influenced by Hull. The expectations are that punishment given by parents under certain conditions will bring about feelings of anxiety and will inhibit wrongdoing, quite independent of whether, in the current situation, the child is punished. Avoidance and inhibition learnt in the home from parents should be generalisable to any and every situation outside even when there is no supervision of the child. Thus the conscience built up through reward and punishment will be taken into all situations. The excellent studies of Hartshorne and May gave little support to these views. Only small correlation coefficients were found between behaviours measuring self-control, service to others, or honesty. The same was found in respect of relationships found between cheating in different situations, e.g. home and school. Rather similar results were found by Sears, Rau and Alpert (111), so it looks as if responses to tests involving moral conduct do depend upon the actual situation to a considerable extent although not completely so. The question of the relationship between moral judgement and moral conduct will be raised separately later in the chapter.

When we say that moral conduct does not seem to be able to be predicted on the basis of learning theory it does not contradict the view expressed by, say, Peck and Havighurst (96) that character seems to be learned. This merely expressed the view that character is affected by other persons and environmental experiences. Indeed it is plain that characters are often changed for the better or for the worse at times. But we do not know the exact processes involved or how to be sure of changing character. So using learning theory in a precise technical sense we cannot predict the development of morality or conscience as measured by resistance to temptation situations.

PSYCHOANALYTIC THEORY AND MORALITY

In Freudian theory the concept of guilt has a very important place and it has wide implications in psychotherapy. The view is, of course, that punitiveness of the parents eventually becomes self-punishment through the build-up of superego. It is argued that there is considerable guilt or capacity for self-punishment in almost all children and adults, and most responses to wrongdoing involve satisfying the need for punishment and self-blame. This anticipation of future self-punishment following wrongdoing or transgression of the rules, serves as a drive for developing resistance to temptation and for behaving in ways which are not at variance with these internalised standards.

It is very difficult to make a direct test of the validity of psychoanalytic theory at this point. In the study by Sears, Rau and Alpert there was, among four-year-olds, little relationship between resistance to temptation and measures of guilt. So the avoidance of self-punishment, remorse, and loss of self-esteem which would follow transgression did not appear to be powerful enough motive for these subjects to resist temptation. Kohlberg (67) in a thorough review of many studies in this area tentatively concludes that psychoanalytic theory is inadequate to explain the evidence relating to guilt responses in the development of the child. He thinks that instead of thinking of guilt in terms of self-punitive

H

reactions derived from an internal unconscious structure, namely the superego, the concept of guilt has far more meaning if thought of as a conscious self-critical and self-controlling response.

ROLE-LEARNING THEORY AND MORALITY

When children find that behaving like persons whom they regard as important to them brings positive results, they are likely to identify with such persons. At least, this is the meaning of the term identification in role-learning theory and is invoked to explain much social learning. On this view the antecedents of strong identification leading to a strong conscience is a sense of dependency upon the persons concerned. Identification thus results because of the child's need of nurturance and continuation of his parents' love; or because of the power he sees his parents possess over resources (e.g. cars, dogs) which he desires, or their power in the field of manipulating people in social relationships. Thus a boy may identify with the father because of the latter's success with the mother.

The study of Sears, Maccoby and Levin discussed earlier, found that in families where there was a warm relationship between parents and children, the withdrawal of love (mother looks hurt, voice quavers, says less than usual) was linked with the child confessing to wrongdoing. This was not so in the case of 'cold' mothers. However, even in the case of 'warm' mothers withdrawal of love did not seem to control moral behaviour generally; it simply elicited one, and only one, symptom of guilt, namely confession to wrongdoing. This study, and others, suggest that moral behaviour is certainly linked with the general quality of the love relationship between parents and children but we do not know if such behaviour is brought about by identification with warm nurturant parents.

A number of workers such as Kagan (61), also Bandura *et al.* (6) have indeed produced evidence which suggests that children envy the power which other persons have over resources and social relationships. Moreover the children are likely to identify with them. However, Kohlberg (67) after reviewing much relevant evidence points out that there is little support for the view that variations in the strength of identification and conscience result from variations in parental power. Perhaps there is a 'ceiling effect' at work in the sense that all parents are so powerful in the eyes of their offspring that variations in parental power are unimportant.

When one considers numbers of children, none of the above theories has been shown to be particularly helpful. But in the case of a specific child, one or more of the theories may be able to offer an explanation of moral development. The work dealt with in the next section is discussed at greater length since the associated evidence does seem to be a little more consistent.

DEVELOPMENTAL APPROACH TO THE ACQUISITION OF MORALITY

The two theories to be discussed here are those of Piaget (99) and Kohlberg (67). The former sees the child's environment as a social situation in which the child increasingly understands the rules by spontaneously restricting his moral experiences in an effort to make them meaningful to him. Through this means external rules become transformed into internal principles. Of course, variations in the social environment can accelerate or retard the process, but for Piaget this is the essential mechanism, and not rewards and punishments or identification.

Piaget has proposed three main stages in the growth of moral judgement. The first, lasting from about four to eight years of age is that of *heteronomy*. Rules and laws are sacred and fixed for all occasions as they have been given by adults and older children. It is the letter rather than the spirit of the law that must be observed. Behaviour will be judged not in terms of the motives which prompted it but by conformity with the rules. When stories are read to children they will make judgements devoid of pity and psychological insight. The child's egocentrism does not allow him to see moral values as relative to the situation; while moral realism – the confusion of subjective phenomena with objective things – gives moral rules as fixed and eternal and not as psychosocial phenomena.

The second stage is one of *equality*. It is permeated by the spirit of equalitarianism. The pupil is no longer dominated by the letter of the rule; rewards and punishments must be distributed equally and the latter must be related to the misdeed. Justice should be reciprocal. When blow is given for blow the child is showing a sense of reciprocity. This stage said to develop out of a growing mutual respect for others. Stage three is one of *equity*. Here we have a relationship based not on mere equality but on the real situation in which each individual may find himself. Thus extenuating circumstances are contemplated and allowances are made for individual motives, needs and deserts.

In a study involving moral judgements in history carried out under the writer's direction, R. N. Hallam (50) found that Piaget's stages did not cover all the answers obtained. Some were so confused that they were judged below the heteronomous level and were classified as 'poor'. But a few answers possessed more complexity than that allowed by Piaget's stage of equity. For our most advanced stage of moral judgement, Tillick's (126) 'theonomy' was taken indicating the most developed ethic for 'man come of age'. There is here a clear difficulty of making moral judgements in some cases since no one is omniscient; no clear cut decisions are sometimes possible; a realisation that neither side in a conflict is completely right; while egocentricity is completely abandoned whether of self, country or creed.

The considerable amount of research that has been carried out on the stages proposed by Piaget supported some of his proposals but not others. Those aspects of his work which involve intellectual growth in the perception of moral values seem to be genuine developmental dimensions as, for example, when the child moves away from believing that his judgement concerning the rightness or wrongness of an act is shared by everyone. Again, social class differences affect only the rate of development since children in all social classes move in the same direction with age. But in other matters such as the relation between the onset of the stage of equality and a growing mutual respect for persons, his conceptual framework has not been consistently validated.

Kohlberg (66) followed in the Piagetian tradition by asking children to judge the morality of conduct found in stories. For example (remember the study was carried out in the USA where there is no National Health Service):

Radium was needed to treat an ill wife. The husband had not the money to purchase this nor could he borrow the money. As his wife was dying he asked the druggist to sell him the radium cheap or let him pay later. The druggist refused. So the man broke into the shop and stole the radium. Should he have done this?

The study revealed, in Kohlberg's view, six developmental stages. While the first two are similar to Piaget's stages of heteronomy and equality, he did not find that unilateral respect for authority and mutual respect between peers as the causes of the hetero-nomous and equalitarian moralities respectively. Moreover it was by using questions more difficult than Piaget used that it was possible to show that moral development continues to 17 years of age. In the sixth stage the young person judges conduct in terms of his own internalised standards and in comparative independence of the social situation. His conscience now makes him do what is right to avoid self-condemnation.

Kohlberg concludes that something like the internalisation of moral rules, or conscience, depends closely upon the cognitive growth of moral concepts, and that conscience develops late. Piagetian, learning and psychoanalytic theories all assume that the basic features of the adult conscience are there by eight years of age. Piaget must assume this because by that age concrete operational thought is in evidence, while the last named also demands an early age if conscience is to be derived through early identification. Kohlberg finds that his levels of moral development correlate ·31 with IQ, but ·59 with chronological age when mental age is held constant. He also found that social class and the extent of participation in peer group activities was also related to moral development quite independently of IQ.

Our work at Leeds into the growth of moral judgements in history shows clearly that the level of development reached in a situation depends upon the intellectual complexity of the situation. In general it is around the sixteenth birthday that adolescents of average ability reach Piaget's stage of equity in respect of moral judgements in history. Other workers have also concluded that many adolescents still judge at the level of equality. It must, of course, be understood that many pupils are willing to discuss moral problems in many and varied situations of life from the age of twelve onwards.

MORAL KNOWLEDGE AND MORAL CONDUCT

Swainson (122) in a study of British children showed that most ten-year-olds had acquired a good deal of moral knowledge. More recently Bradburn (12) showed that among a large number of ten-year-olds the following kinds of behaviour were generally considered bad conduct: dishonesty, irresponsible action, damage to property, cruelty to animals and old people. These British children have a well developed conscience in the sense that they know what is regarded as right and wrong. The question that causes so much perplexity is why it is that moral conduct does not keep pace with moral knowledge. It is, of course, impossible to answer this satisfactorily at the moment. Perhaps we have a parallel instance in the case where one has a profound intellectual grasp of some political or theological system but our actions are often little affected. In the case of moral knowledge and political/theological knowledge it is certain that it is intellectual growth that helps us to understand the issues involved, but there is a failure, as it were, in the motivational system. Nevertheless a brief perusal of the relevant literature relating to moral knowledge and moral conduct is important.

Hartshorne and May obtained a score for moral knowledge. Among 11-12-year-olds they found a correlation coefficient of ·34 between this score and the total score obtained on character as measured in the experimental situation. The corresponding figure between the score on ratings of good character by teachers and peers, and total score for moral knowledge, was ·43. Kohlberg related his levels of moral judgement to moral conduct. The correlation between these levels and teacher judgements were ·51 for fairness to peers, and ·31 for 'conscience'. He also claims that there is a moderate correlation between level of moral judgement and the ability to withstand pressure from others to change or violate one's moral beliefs, while a test of cheating picked out those who were high and low in respect of level of judgement.

Moral conduct thus does seem to be linked with moral judgement which in turn is related to cognitive growth and social experience, as we saw earlier. The effects of social experience can range from, say, the giving of experience of the results of wrongdoing, to the changing of the self-concept. Intelligence gives the individual insight into the antecedents of the present situation, the situation itself, and the probable long-term outcomes of given actions.

But it must not be thought from what was said in the last paragraph that the relationships between moral conduct and cognitive growth coupled with social experience is high. Although the correlation coefficients are only modest in size, they are more consistent than are other measures that have been related to conduct. They leave plenty of room for able and experienced people to be immoral, and for the less able with limited experience to have high standards of behaviour. Other influences are also relevant. For example, trait theories of personality recognise a dimension of dependability versus undependability or ego-strength versus neuroticism. It is characterised by such traits as reliability and emotional stability versus their opposites. This dimension is in part genetically determined (14). One must recognise, therefore, that constitutional factors are at work in many situations demanding moral choice. Such factors will determine, to some extent, how well moral judgements result in moral conduct in specific situations where, say, ability to tolerate frustration is involved, or where the individual is up against the operation of a natural tendency, e.g. hunger. Again, the strength of a current psychological need (e.g. to receive recognition, or to maintain one's self picture) will also influence the extent to which temptation can be resisted and conduct be moral. Long ago Washbourne (133) concluded that a good character possessed 'impulse judgement', that is, the ability to weigh an immediate satisfaction against a future satisfaction and arrive at a decision as to which of the two is the more desirable. Thus constitutional influences, the degree to which a particular situation is one of temptation to an individual, as well as moral knowledge, are all factors which determine moral conduct.

Peck and Havighurst (96) studied character development in a group of children in a small mid-western town in the USA in which there was little segregation by social class and no social disorganisation. They found that children who had the best self-control at 10 years of age tended to be the best self-controlled individuals at 16. Those adolescents with the highest degree of moral stability were found to have families in which the rearing was characterised by: consistency of standards and guidance, trust and love, a democratic atmosphere, and punishments which were not severe. While parents encouraged their children to make decisions, they always reserved for themselves the right to have the final word if necessary. Peck and Havighurst do not say so, but it would appear that even in this community genetic influences were at work. Parents who can adopt and maintain such methods in child rearing are probably stable and well adjusted themselves.

FURTHER READING

Breznitz, S. and Kugelmass, S. 'Intentionality in Moral Judgment: Developmental Stages', *Child Developm.*, 38, 469–79 (1967)

Edwards, J. B. 'Some Studies of the Moral Development of Children', *Educational Research*, 7, 200–211 (1965)

Eysenck, H. J. 'The Development of Moral Values in Children. VII – The Contribution of Learning Theory', *Brit. J. Educ. Psychol.* 30, 11–21 (1960)

Graham, D. 'Children's Moral Development', *Educational Research in Britain* (Ed. Butcher, J.) (London, University of London Press 1968)

Hillard, F. H. 'The Influence of Religious Education upon the Development of Children's Moral Ideas', *Brit. J. Educ. Psychol.*, 29, 50–9 (1959)

Kaufer, F. H. and Duerfeldt, P. H. 'Age, Class Standing and Commitments as Determinants of Cheating in Children', *Child Developm.*, 39, 545–57 (1968)

Kay, W. *Moral Developments* (Allen and Unwin 1968)

Morris, J. F. 'The Development of Adolescent Value Judgments', *Brit. J. Educ. Psychol.*, 28, 1–14 (1958)

Peters, R. S. 'Freud's Theory of Moral Development in Relation to that of Piaget', *Brit. J. Educ. Psychol.*, 30, 250–8 (1960)

Porteus, B. D. and Johnson, R. C. 'Children's Responses to Two Measures of Conscience Development and their Relation to Sociometric Nomination', *Child Developm.*, 36, 703–11 (1965)

Pringle, M. L. K. and Edwards, J. B. 'Some Moral Concepts and Judgments of Junior School Children', *Brit. J. Soc. Clin. Psychol.*, 3, 196–215 (1964)

Turiel, E. 'An Experimental Test of the Sequentiality of Developmental Stages in the Child's Moral Judgments', *J. Per. Soc. Psychol.*, 3, 611–18 (1966)

Bibliography

1. Allport, F. H. *Theories of Perception and the Concept of Structure* (Wiley 1955)
2. Allport, G. W. *Personality. A Psychological Interpretation* (Constable 1937)
3. Ammons, R. B. & Holmes, J. C. 'The Full-Scale Vocabulary Test: Results for a Pre-School Population', *Child Developm.* **20**, 5–14 (1949)
4. Auerbach, C. *Heredity* (Oliver & Boyd 1965)
5. Ausubel, D. P. 'Maturation and Learning in Human Development', *Int. J. Educ. Sci.*, **1**, 47–60 (1966)
6. Bandura, A., Ross, D. & Ross, S. A. 'A Comparative Test of the Status Envy, Social Power, and Reinforcement Theories of Identificatory Learning', *J. abnorm. soc. Psychol.*, **67**, 527–34 (1963)
7. Barry, H. A., Child, I. L. & Bacon, M. K. 'Relation of Child-Training to Subsistence Economy' *Am. Anthrop.*, **61**, 51–63 (1959)
8. Bayley, N. & Schaefer, E. S. 'Correlations of Maternal and Child Behaviours with the Development of Mental Abilities', *Monogr. Soc. Res. Child Developm.*, **29** (6) (1964)
9. Berko, J. 'The Child's Learning of English Morphology' *Word*, **14**, 150–77 (1958)
10. Bernstein, B. 'Aspects of Language and Learning in the Genesis of the Social Process' *J. Child Psychol. Psychiat.*, **1**, 313–24 (1961)
11. Birch, H. G. & Belmont, L. 'Auditory-Visual Integration in Normal and Retarded Readers', *Am. J. Orthopsychiat.*, **34**, 852–61
12. Bradburn, E. 'Children's Moral Knowledge', *Educ. Res.*, **9**, 203–7 (1967)
13. Braine, M. D. S. 'The Ontogeny of English Phrase Structure', *Language*, **39**, 1–13 (1963)
14. Bronson, W. C. 'Central Orientations: A Study of Behaviour Organization from Childhood through Adolescence', *Child Developm.*, **37**, 125–55 (1966)
15. Brown, R. & Bellugi, U. 'Three Processes in the Child's Acquisition of Syntax', *Harv. educat. Rev.*, **34**, 133–51 (1964)
16. Brown, R., Cazden, C. & Bellugi, U. 'The Child's Grammar

from I to III', *Minnesota Symposia on Child Psychology*, **2** (Minneapolis, University of Minnesota Press 1969)

17. Bruner, J. S. Olver, R. R. & Greenfield, P. M. (Eds.) *Studies in Cognitive Growth* (Wiley 1966)

18. Burks, B. S. 'On the Relative Contributions of Nature and Nurture to Average Group Differences in Intelligence', *Proc. natn. Acad. Sci.*, **24**, 276–82 (1938)

19. Burns, D. G. *Vocabulary of the Secondary School Child* (National Foundation for Educational Research 1960)

20. Burt, C. 'The Evidence for the Concept of Intelligence', *Br. J. Educ. Psychol.*, **25**, 158–77 (1955)

21. Campbell, A. 'St Thomas Negroes – a Study of Personality and Culture', *Psychol. Monogr.*, **55**, (5) (1943)

22. Cattell, R. B. *The Scientific Analysis of Personality* (Pelican A712 1965)

22A. Cazden, C. B. 'The Acquisition of Noun and Verb Inflections', *Child Developm.*, **39**, 433–48 (1968)

23. Chomsky, N. *Aspects of the Theory of Syntax* (Cambridge, M.I.T. Press 1965)

24. Cloward, R. A. & Ohlin, L. E. *Delinquency and Opportunity* (Glencoe Free Press 1955)

25. Cohen, A. K. *Delinquent Boys: The Culture of the Gang* (Glencoe Free Press 1955)

25A. Deregowski, J. B. 'Difficulties in Depth Perception in Africa', *Brit. J. Psychol.*, **59**, 195–204 (1968)

26. Dodwell, P. C. 'Relations between the Understanding of the Logic of Classes and of Cardinal Number in Children', *Can. J. Psychol.*, **16**, 152–60 (1962)

27. Dollard, J. & Miller, N. E. *Personality and Psychotherapy* (McGraw Hill 1950)

28. Donaldson, M. in *Psycholinguistic Papers* (Eds. Lyons, J. & Wales, R. J.) (Edinburgh University Press 1966)

29. Drever, J. *A Dictionary of Psychology* (Penguin Reference Books 1952)

30. Erickson, E. H. *Childhood and Society* (W. W. Norton 1950)

31. Erickson, E. H. 'Identity and the Life Cycle: Selected Papers', *Psychol. Issues* (International Press 1958)

32. Erickson, E. H. 'The Problem of Ego Identity', *J. Am. psychoanal. Ass.*, **4**, 56–121 (1956)

33. Erickson, E. H. *Symposium on the Healthy Personality* (Ed. Senn, M. J. E.) (Josiah Macy Jr. Foundation 1950)

34. Fantz, R. L. 'The Origin of Form Perception', *Scientific American*, **204**, 66–72 (1961)

35. Fantz, R. L. 'Pattern Vision in Newborn Infants', *Science*, **140**, 296–7 (1963)

36. Fantz, R. L., Ordy, J. M., & Udelf, M. S. 'Maturation of Pattern Vision in Infants during the First Six Months', *J. comp. physiol. Psychol.*, **55**, 907–17 (1967)

37. Fisher, G. H. 'Developmental Features of Behaviour and Perception', *J. educ. Psychol.*, **35**, 69–78 (1965)

38. Flavell, J. H. *The Developmental Psychology of Jean Piaget* (Van Nostrand 1963)

39. Fraser, C., Bellugi, U. & Brown, R. 'Control of Grammar in Imitation, Comprehension and Production', *J. verb. Learn. verb. Behav.*, **2**, 121–35 (1963)

40. Freud, A. *The Ego and the Mechanisms of Defence* (Hogarth 1937)

41. Freud, S. *Basic Writings of S. Freud* (Ed. Brill, A. A.) (Random House 1938)

42. Furth, H. *Thinking without Language* (Glencoe Free Press 1966)

43. Galperin, P. Y. 'A Method, Facts and Theories in the Psychology of Mental Actions and Concept Formation', Paper read at the 18th International Congress of Psychology (Moscow 1966)

44. Gibson, E. J. in 'Basic Cognitive Processes' (Eds. Wright, J. C. & Kagan, J.), *Monogr. Soc. Res. Child Developm.* **28**, (2) (1963)

45. Gottesman, I. I. 'Genetic Variance in Adaptive Personality Traits', *J. Child Psychol. Psychiat.*, **7**, 199–208 (1966)

46. Greenberg, J. H. in *Universals of Language* (Ed. Greenberg, J. H.) (M.I.T. Press, 2nd Edition 1966)

47 Hall, C. S. *A Primer of Freudian Psychology* (World Publishing Co. 1954)

48. Hall, C. S. & Lindzey, G. *Theories of Personality* (Wiley 1957)

49. Hallam, R. N. 'Logical Thinking in History', *Educ. Rev.*, **19**, 183–202 (1967)

50. Hallam, R. N. *An Investigation into some Aspects of the Historical Thinking of Children and Adolescents* (M.Ed. Thesis, University of Leeds 1966)

51. Hartshorne, H. & May, M. A. *Studies in Deceit* (Macmillan 1928)

52. Hebb, D. O. *The Organisation of Behaviour* (Chapman and Hall 1949)

53. Hilgard, E. R. 'Human Motives and Concept of the Self', *Am. Psychol.*, **4**, 374–82 (1949)

54. Hilgard, E. R. *Introduction to Psychology* (Methuen 1962)

55. Hockberg J. & Brooks, V. 'Pictorial Recognition as an Unlearned Ability', *Am. J. Psychol.*, **75**, 624–8 (1962)

56. Hudson, W. 'Pictorial Depth Perception in Sub-Cultural Groups in Africa', *J. Soc. Psychol.*, **52**, 183–208 (1960)

57. Hull, C. L. 'The Conflicting Psychologies of Learning – A Way Out', *Psychol. Rev.* **42**, 491–516 (1935)

58. Hull, C. L. *Principles of Behaviour* (Appleton-Century-Crofts 1943)

59. Inhelder, B., Bovet, M., Sinclair, H. & Smock, C. D. 'On Cognitive Development', *American Psychologist,* **21**, 160–4 (1966)

60. Inhelder, B. & Piaget, J. *The Growth of Logical Thinking* (Routledge and Kegan Paul 1958)

61. Kagan, J. 'The Concept of Identification', *Psychol. Rev.* **60**, 296–305 (1958)

62. Kagan, J., Hoshen, B. & Watson, S. 'The Child's Symbolic Conceptualization of the Parents', *Child Developm.,* **32**, 625–36 (1961)

63. Kagan, J. & Moss, H. A. *Birth to Maturity* (Wiley 1962)

64. Kidd, A. H. & Kidd, R. N. in *Perceptual Development in Children* (Eds. Kidd, A. H. and Rivoire, J. L.) (University of London Press 1967)

65. Klima, E. S. & Bellugi, U. in *Psycholinguistic Papers* (Eds. Lyons, J. and Wales, R. J.) (University of Edinburgh Press 1966)

66. Kohlberg, L. 'The Development of Children's Orientations toward a Moral Order', *Vita Humana,* **6**, 11–33 (1963)

67. Kohlberg, L. in 'Child Psychology', *National Society for the Study of Education,* Part 1 (1963)

68. Kohn, M. L. 'Social Class and Parental Values', *Am. J. Sociology,* **64**, 337–51 (1959)

69. Kohn, M. L. 'Social Class and the Exercise of Parental Authority' *Am. Sociological Rev.,* **24**, 352–66 (1959)

70. Laurendeau, M. & Pinard, A. *Causal Thinking in the Child* (International Universities Press 1962)

71. Lenneberg, E. H. in 'The Acquisition of Language' (Eds. Bellugi, U. and Brown, R.), *Monogr. Soc. Res. Child Developm.,* **29** (1) (1964)

72. Lenneberg, E. H. *Biological Foundations of Language,* (Wiley 1967)

73. Lewis, M. M. *Infant Speech* (Routledge and Kegan Paul 1951)

74. Linton, R. *The Cultural Background of Personality* (Appleton-Century-Crofts 1945)

75. Lovell, K. 'A Follow Up of some aspects of the Work of Piaget and Inhelder into the Child's Conception of Space', *Br. J. educ. Psychol.,* **29**, 104–17 (1959)

76. Lovell, K. 'A Follow Up Study of Inhelder and Piaget's The Growth of Logical Thinking', *Br. J. Psychol.,* **52**, 143–54 (1961)

77. Lovell, K. *The Growth of Basic Mathematical and Scientific Concepts in Children* (University of London Press 1966)

78. Lovell, K. & Bradbury, B. 'The Growth of English Morphology in ESN Special School Children', *Am. J. ment. Defic.,* **71**, 609–15 (1967)

79. Lovell, K. & Butterworth, I. B. 'Abilities Underlying the

Understanding of Proportionality', *Mathematics Teaching*, No. 37, 5-9 (1966)

80. Lovell, K. & Dixon, E. 'The Growth of the Control of Grammar in Imitation, Comprehension and Production', *J. Child Psychol. Psychiat.*, **8**, 31-9 (1967)

81. Lovell, K. & Gorton, A. 'A Study of some Differences between Backward and Normal Readers of Average Intelligence', *Br. J. Educ. Psychol.*, **38**, 240-48 (1968)

82. Lovell, K., Hoyle, H. W. & Siddall, M. Q. 'A Study of Some Aspects of the Play and Language of Young Children with Delayed Speech', *J. Child Psychol. Psychiat.*', **9**, 41-50 (1968)

83. Lunzer, E. A. in 'European Research in Cognitive Development' (Ed. Mussen, P.), *Monogr. Soc. Res. Child Developm.*, **30**, (2) (1965)

84. Luria, A. R. in *Educational Psychology in the Soviet Union* (Eds. Simon, B. and Simon, J.) (Routledge and Kegan Paul 1963)

85. McCarthy, D. in *Manual of Child Psychology* (Ed. Carmichael, L.) (Chapman and Hall 1954)

86. McNeill, D. in *The Genesis of Language* (M.I.T. Press 1966)

87. Malinowski, B. *The Sexual Life of Savages in Northwestern Melanesia* (Liveright 1929)

88. Mead, M. *Sex and Temperament in Three Primitive Societies* (Morrow 1935)

89. Mead, M. 'Character Formation in Two South Seas Societies', *Proc. Am. Neurol. Assn.*, **66**, 99-103 (1940)

89A. Menyuk, P. 'Syntactic Structures in the Language of Children', *Child Developm.*, **34**, 407-22 (1963)

89B. Menyuk, P. 'Syntactic Rules Used by Children from Preschool through First Grade', *Child Developm.*, **35**, 533-46 (1964)

90. Miller, W. B. 'Lower Class Culture as a Generating Milieu of Gang Delinquency', *J. of Social Issues*, **16**, 5-19 (1958)

91. Miller, W. & Ervin, S. in 'The Acquisition of Language', *Monogr. Soc. Res. Child Developm.*, **29** (1) (1964)

92. Money, J. 'Cytogenetic and Psychosexual Incongruities with a Note on Space-Form Blindness', *Am. J. Psychiat.*, **119**, 820-27 (1963)

93. Moore, T. 'Language and Intelligence: A Longitudinal Study of the First Eight Years', *Human Development*, **10**, 88-106 (1967)

94. Mussen, P. H. & Bouterline-Young, H. 'Relationships between Rate of Maturing and Personality among boys of Italian Descent', *Vita Humana*, **7**, 186-200 (1964)

95. Pasamanick, B. & Knobloch, H. 'Retrospective Studies on the Epidemiology of Reproductive Causality: Old and New' (*Merrill-Palmer Quarterly*, **12**, 7-26 (1966)

96. Peck, R. F. & Havighurst, R. J. *The Psychology of Character Development* (Wiley 1960)

97. Peluffo, N. 'La nozione di conservazione del volume e le operazioni di combinazioni come induce di sviluppo del pensiero operatorio in soggetti appartenenti ad ambienti fisici e socioculturali diversi', *Rivista di Psicologia Sociale*, 2-3, 99-132 (1964)

98. Piaget, J. *The Language and Thought of the Child* (Kegan Paul, Trench, Trubner 1926)

99. Piaget, J. *The Moral Judgment of the Child* (Kegan Paul 1932)

100. Piaget, J. *The Psychology of Intelligence* (Routledge and Kegan Paul 1950)

101. Piaget, J. 'Le développement de la perception de l'enfant à l'adulte', *Bull. Psychol.*, 8, (183) (1954-5)

102. Piaget, J. *The Origins of Intelligence in Children* (Routledge and Kegan Paul 1952)

103. Piaget, J. & Inhelder, B. *The Child's Conception of Space* (Routledge and Kegan Paul 1956)

104. Piaget, J. & Morf, A. 'Les "préinférences" perceptives et leurs relations avec les schèmes sensori-moteurs et opératoires'. In *Etudes d'épistémologie génétique*, 6 (Presses Univer. France 1958)

105. Pronko, N. H., Ebert, R. & Greenberg, G. in *Perceptual Development in Children* (Eds. Kidd, A. H. and Rivoire, J. L.) (University of London Press 1967)

106. Rivoire, J. L. & Kidd, A. H. in *Perceptual Development in Children* (Eds. Kidd, A. H. and Rivoire, J. L.) (University of London Press 1967)

107. Rogers, C. R. *On Becoming a Person: A Therapist's View of Psychotherapy* (Houghton Mifflin 1961)

108. Sapir, E. *Language, an Introduction to the Study of Speech* (Harcourt Brace 1921)

109. Schaefer, E. S. & Bayley, N. 'Maternal Behaviour, Child Behaviour, and their Intercorrelations from Infancy through Adolescence', *Monogr. Soc. Res. in Child Developm.*, 28 (3) (1963)

110. Sears, R. R., Maccoby, E. E. & Levin, H. *Patterns of Child Rearing* (Row Paterson 1957)

111. Sears, R. R., Rau, L. & Alpert, R. *Identification and Child Rearing* (Tavistock Publications 1966)

112. Sewell, W. H. 'Social Class and Childhood Personality', *Sociometry*, 24, 340-56 (1961)

113. Sherif, M. & Sherif, C. W. *An Outline of Social Psychology* (Harper, Revised Edition 1956)

114. Shields, J. *Monozygotic Twins* (Oxford University Press 1962)

115. Skeels, H. M. 'Adult Status of Children with Contrasting Early

Life Experiences', *Monogr. Soc. Res. Child. Developm.*, **31** (3) (1966)

116. Smith, M. E. 'An Investigation of the Development of the Sentence and the Extent of the Vocabulary of Young Children', *Univ. Iowa Stud. Child Welf.*, **3** (1926)

117. Smith, M. K. 'Measurement of the Size of General English Vocabulary through the Elementary Grades and the High School', *Genet. Psychol. Monogr.*, **24,** 311–45 (1941)

118. Staats, A. W. & Staats, C. K. *Complex Human Behaviour* (Holt, Rinehart & Winston 1963)

119. Stott, D. H. 'Evidence for a Congenital Factor in Maladjustment and Delinquency', *Am. J. Psychiat.*, **118,** 781–94 (1962)

120. Stott, D. H. *Studies of Troublesome Children* (Tavistock 1966)

121. Sutherland, N. S. in *Psycholinguistic Papers* (Edinburgh University Press, 1966)

122. Swainson, B. M. *The Development of Moral Ideas in Children and Adolescents* (Ph.D. Thesis, Oxford 1949)

123. Sydow, Von G. & Rinne, A. 'Very Unequal "Identical" Twins', *Acta Pediat.*, **67,** 163–71 (1958)

124. Tanner, J. *Education and Physical Growth* (University of London Press 1961)

125. Templin, M. C. *Certain Language Skills in Children* (Oxford University Press 1957)

126. Tillick, Q. *The Protestant Era* (Nisbet, 1951)

127. Vandenberg, S. G. 'The Hereditary Abilities Study: Hereditary Components in a Psychological Test Battery', *Am. J. hum. Genet.* **14**, 220–37 (1962)

128. Vernon, M. D. *Backwardness in Reading* (Cambridge University Press 1957)

129. Vurpillot, E. 'Piaget's Law of Relative Centrations', *Acta psychol.*, **16**, 403–30 (1959)

130. Vygotsky, L. S. *Thought and Language* (Wiley 1962)

131. Walk, R. D. & Gibson, E. J. 'A Comparative and Analytic Study of Visual Depth Perception', *Psychol. Monogr.*, **75** (Whole number 519) (1961)

132. Wallace, J. G. *Concept Growth and the Education of the Child* (National Foundation for Educational Research 1965)

133. Washbourne, J. N. 'Definitions in Character Measurement', *J. Soc. Psychol.*, **1**, 114–119 (1931)

134 Watts, A. F. *The Language and Mental Development of Children* (Harrap 1948)

135. Whiting, J. W. M. & Child, I. L. *Child Training and Personality: A Cross Cultural Study* (Yale University Press 1953)

136. Whiting, J. W. M. & Whiting, B. B. in *Handbook of Research Methods in Child Development* (Wiley 1960)

137. Witkin, H. A. *et al. Personality through Perception* (Harper 1954)

138. Wiseman, S. *Education and Environment* (Manchester University Press 1964)

139. Wohlwill, J. F. 'Developmental Studies of Perception', *Psychol. Bull.*, **57,** 249–88 (1960)

140. Wursten, H. 'Recherches sur le développement des perceptions. IX', *Arch. Psychol.*, **32,** 1–144 (1947–9)

141. Yarrow, L. J. 'Maternal Deprivation: Toward an Empirical and Conceptual Revaluation', *Psychol. Bull.*, **58,** 459–90 (1961)

I

Glossary

ACCOMMODATION. In Piaget's system the term implies the modification of intellectual structures by new experiences or the build up of new structures.

ADAPTATION. The process of becoming more effectively adjusted to the on-going environmental conditions.

ASSIMILATION. In Piaget's system the term implies the absorption and integration of new experiences into previously organised intellectual structures.

AUTISTIC THINKING. Mental activity controlled by the wishes of the individual, as contrasted with the real nature of the situation.

CELL. The basic unit out of which living organisms are built.

CHROMOSOMES. Dark bodies of various shapes and sizes arranged in pairs within the nucleus of the cell. They carry the determiners of hereditary traits.

CORRELATION COEFFICIENT. A measure of the degree of agreement between two variables varying from $+1.0$ (perfect agreement) to -1.0. (complete disagreement).

CYTOPLASM. A relatively clear substance separated from the nucleus of the cell by the nuclear membrane.

DNA. Deoxyribonucleic acid, or the information-carrying material of which the genes are composed.

EGO. In the Freudian sense it is that part of the personality which is conscious and which represents external reality to the person through the senses. Its task is to hold a balance beween the strivings of the id, the censure of the superego and the demands of reality.

EGOCENTRIC SPEECH. Speech in which the speaker makes no attempt to adapt the speech to the needs of the listener or even to make sure he is listening.

EPISTEMOLOGY. The theory or science of the method or ground of knowledge.

EQUILIBRIUM. A state in which a system has some kind of balance or stability with respect to the forces acting upon or within it.

GAMETE. A mature male or female reproductive cell – sperm and ovum respectively.

GENE. A unit of DNA located on a chromosome. Genes control developmental processes.

GENOTYPE. Genetical constitution as determined by the total of the genes present in the individual.

HAPTIC. Relating to the sense of touch.

ID. Term used by Freud to indicate that part of the personality consisting of instinctual drives and almost wholly within the unconscious.

ISOMORPHIC. Relating to corresponding structures.

MATURATION. Development that is attributable to genetic and/or incidental experience.

MORPHEME. The smallest element in speech to which meaning can be assigned.

NUCLEI. Plural form of nucleus. The latter is the rather dense stainable body inside the cell containing the chromosomes. It is surrounded by the cytoplasm.

OPERATIONS. A term used by Piaget to indicate mental actions which form an integral part of an organised network of related actions.

ORGANISATION. Relating to the systems of relationships between elements.

PHENOTYPE. The totality of the observable characteristics of an organism. It is the product of the interaction between the genotype and the environment.

PRIMARY CIRCULAR REACTION. Type of behaviour displayed by the young infant when neonatal reflexes start to change and alter their form as a function of experience. Thus sucking is part of an innate reflex, but systematic thumb-sucking is acquired.

REFLEX. The direct and immediate response of a muscle or gland to the stimulation of a sense organ.

REGULATIONS. Partial and momentary compensations which are midway between irreversible centrations and reversible operations.

SCHEMA. Term used by Piaget to indicate a series of actions which have both sequence and structure. In the post infancy period mental actions are involved. Thus in the early days of life we may speak of the schema of sucking; in adolescence of the schema of proportion.

SECONDARY CIRCULAR REACTION. Behaviour in which the child attempts to maintain, through repetition, interesting changes brought about in the environment – external to his body – which were first produced by chance.

SOCIALISE. The bringing of the child to the position where he behaves in a way appropriate to his place in society.

SOCIALISED SPEECH. Speech made with the clear intention to

communicate and to make or persuade the listener to adopt some course of action.

SUPEREGO. A term to indicate that part of the personality which results mainly from the child's interactions with his parents and other adults. The superego acts as a kind of conscience and criticises the thought and actions of the ego, and is found largely within the unconscious.

SYMBOLIC FUNCTION. The capacity of the child to differentiate between a signifier (e.g. an image or a word) and that which the signifier represents, and to make an act of reference.

TERTIARY CIRCULAR REACTION. Behaviour in which an action is repeated again and again although not in a mechanical way, but rather by playing variations upon the theme and deliberately trying to vary it.

ZYGOTE. Fertilised ovum produced by the union of male and female gametes.

Index

language (*cont.*)
  early grammars, 60 ff.
  in the first year, 56–58
  innate basis of, 55
  maturation and onset of, 55
  of speech retarded children, 67,
    71
  role of adult speech in, 69, 70
  role of imitation in, 57
  universals, 64
  use of negatives in, 65
Laurendeau, M., and Pinard, A.,
  32, 125
Lenneberg, E. H., 55–56, 57, 125
Lewis, M. M., 56–57, 76, 125
Lindzey, G., 109
Linton, R., 85, 125
logical thought, growth of, 21 ff.
Lovell, K., 32, 35, 49, 67, 125
Lovell, K., and Bradbury, N., 69,
  125
Lovell, K., and Butterworth, I. B.,
  125
Lovell, K., and Dixon, E., 71, 126
Lovell, K., and Gorton, A., 48,
  126
Lovell, K., Hoyle, H. W., and
  Siddall, M. Q., 67, 126
Lunzer, E. A., 33, 126
Luria, A. R., 75, 126
Luria, A. R., and Yudovitch,
  F. I. A., 76

McCarthy, D., 56, 66, 126
McCary, J. L., 95
McNeill, D., 55, 62, 64, 68, 70, 71,
  76, 126
Maier, H. W., 38, 95
Malinowski, B., 96, 126
maturation, 19, 20
Mead, M., 96, 98, 126
Menyuk, P., 64
Merrill, F. E., 109
Miller, W., and Ervin, S., 61, 69,
  126
Miller, W. B., 106, 126

Money, J., 15, 126
Moore, T., 74, 126
moral knowledge and moral conduct, 118–120
morality
  definition of, 111
  developmental approach to,
    115–118
  learning theory and, 112–113
  psychoanalytic theory and, 113–
    114
  role theory and, 114–115
morphology, growth of, 67–68
Morris, J. F., 120
Munn, N. L., 54
Murphy, G., 95
Mussen, P. H., and Bouterline-
  Young, H., 126

neonatal period, 9, 10
Newcombe, T. M., and Hartley,
  E. L., 109

operational thought
  concrete, 29–32
  formal, 32–35

parental conditions, influence on
  behaviour, 17, 18
Pasamanick, B., and Knobloch,
  H., 126
Pavlov, I. P., 81
Peck, R. F., and Havighurst, R. J.,
  113, 120, 127
Peel, E. A., 38
Peluffo, N., 34, 38, 127
perception, 40 ff.
perception in the school situation,
  50 ff.
personality development and
  child-rearing patterns, 99–
    101
  cultural influences, 96–98
  deviant behaviours, 105–107